JOHNNY GET YOUR GUN

JOHNNY GET YOUR GUN

A Personal Narrative of the Somme, Ypres and Arras

JOHN F. TUCKER

WILLIAM KIMBER · LONDON

First published in 1978 by
WILLIAM KIMBER & CO. LIMITED
Godolphin House, 22a Queen Anne's Gate,
London, SW1H 9AE

ISBN 0 7183 0475 6

Photoset in Great Britain by
Specialised Offset Services Limited, Liverpool
and printed by
The Pitman Press, Bath

Contents

List of Illustrations

Acknowledgements

I must first acknowledge the debt I owe to my wife Lilian, who originally encouraged me to put these experiences in writing. In 1914 she was one of the little girls watching over the walls of her school at Sudbury as my battalion one day marched past on the way to Harrow; neither of us aware that we were to meet and marry about ten years later. Our daughters Pamela and Joan have also given me much help and encouragement. Pamela accompanied me on a short trip to France, where we paid hurried visits to St Omer, Arras, and Amiens, including the site at Beaurains where I was wounded. She has spent valuable hours in searching for and obtaining official war maps and in vetting the manuscript and rendering advice and help with the design for the book-jacket.

I am so grateful for the kindness shown by Miss Monica Dickens, her sister Mrs Doris Danby, and cousin Mr Charles Cedric Dickens, who have gone to so much trouble in searching for and eventually finding the print of the cross which I inscribed for their uncle Major C.C. Dickens.

Thanks are also due to Mr Albert Oborn for the photograph of the cross of his brother Sergeant F.S. Oborn. Mr S.G. (Stan) White, MBE, formerly Hon Sec of the Kensington OCA has been most helpful in providing photographs. Miss V.M. Palmer and Mr F.W. Milsom kindly made excellent copies of several photographs for reproduction. I am also most grateful to Mr Norman Sewell who supplied much valuable data without which it would have been difficult to have drawn my map in such detail.

My publishers Messrs William Kimber & Co. Ltd., (in the person of Ms Amy Howlett and Mr Oliver Colman) have my grateful thanks for the kindly guidance and advice given during the production of this volume.

Above all I make humble acknowledgement to the millions who participated with such fortitude in the holocaust of the so-called Great War.

JOHN FRANCIS TUCKER

January 1978
Wembley

Foreword

This is the narrative of a young man's life during the four years of the Great War from 1914 to 1918. It is by no means intended as a war history, which could better be derived from official and other sources, but it is a purely personal experience as remembered after an interval of about sixty years. During this period isolated incidents have come to mind from time to time in most vivid form, exactly as experienced and in great detail, without exaggeration or addition of any kind. Recently having been presented with a tape-recorder I decided to dictate a few such reminiscences and to my surprise found that long forgotten memories were being brought to the surface and followed each other in a more or less consecutive manner. As fluent speech has never been easy with me, I commenced putting my story into writing, with the ensuing result.

With the exception of a few quoted official statements, confirmation of several dates and reference to sketch maps to recall place names, the narrative is almost wholly from my own memory and conclusions.

In my efforts to present a true picture of events some of my statements may possibly cause offence to particular individuals, but I believe that in any such cases the facts have already been fully publicised.

Some of the details may be gruesome and distressing, but I have felt that my story would be incomplete or even misleading had they been omitted.

I must be forgiven if many of the episodes are not strictly in their true sequence, time having tended to misplace some occurrences. Also during some of the major battles movements and operations sometimes became so frequent and involved that it is now almost impossible to recall them in proper sequence. Indeed the physical and mental stresses were at times so great as to leave little impression on the mind. It will also be understood that the infantry soldier often did not know much of what was going on around him beyond the space of a few yards. We had no maps and relied mostly on hearsay and rumour. Of the ten men shown in the two group photographs reproduced in this book eight became casualties from wounds. This gives some indication of the losses sustained by the infantry.

The area covered in these reminiscences stretched over the whole length of the British line, from Ypres to the Somme and included operations on almost all sectors.

The excitement and heroics of my childhood imagination have subsided and left me with the realities and disillusionment of war, the fears, horrors, filth and stench. Now that I have recorded my memories perhaps the ghosts will rest.

I

Diversion – The Awakening

I was about 17½ years old when the Great War broke out, while I was spending the August Bank Holiday 1914 at Brighton. We all thought it would be a short and sharp war, but after about two months it was obvious that it was going to be a long drawn out affair. My cousin Frankie Jones had gone out to France with the first contingent as a sergeant in the Grenadier Guards. His father, a former staff sergeant and a veteran of the South African War, went out early on as a captain in a Suffolk territorial battalion, but was soon wounded and returned to England for discharge.

Appeals were being made for volunteers to reinforce our small Expeditionary Force, and men of all ages were turning up at the recruiting stations in tens of thousands. Morale and patriotism were marvellously high. The great majority of the British public was tremendously proud of our heritage and of our enormous world-wide Empire. The greatest incentive was of course the determination to protect our families and homes from foreign invasion. The possibility of defeat was not for one moment entertained, so great was our faith and trust in our Nation. Spirits were high and much encouragement was given by the popular songs of the time, such as:

Where are the lads of the village tonight
Where are the lads we know.
In Piccadilly or Leicester Square?
No my child, no not there.
They've taken a trip to the Continent
With their rifles and their bayonets bright,
Facing danger gladly, where they're needed badly
That's where they are tonight.

I was under age at the time and had a disability in my rib-cage, which made sustained effort such as long distance running or football difficult, causing much shortness of breath. It was not very likely at that time that I would be accepted in a regular battalion. I felt however that it was up to me to take my place beside those who were sacrificing life and limb to protect our homes, families and country from the enemy. I therefore decided to try a Territorial unit where standards were not so high. As my family had associations with the Kensington Battalion, 13th London Regiment, my father and two uncles having been sergeants in the old Volunteer days, I determined to try and join this.

I would like to say here that military matters were something of an obsession with me. My earliest memories were of the Boer War, and I was intrigued with the fine figure and uniform of my uncle Frank on his return from war. Also I spent many a holiday in the Guards' barracks in the Tower of London, Wellington Barracks, Windsor and Aldershot, seeing the fine parades and brilliant uniforms and getting an insight into the everyday life of the British soldier in peace-time. Much of my reading time was devoted to studying the history of British battles, both ancient and modern. I had also gained some elementary knowledge of drill and the handling of a rifle in the Lads' Brigade. The strict discipline of army life appealed to me, as did the sport, particularly boxing at which I attained some small skill.

My employers were a firm of East Indian export agents in the Strand, where I was working as a junior clerk. Office life was repugnant to me and I would have enjoyed better an outdoor existence, or to be in a more interesting occupation, but my father preferred my working in an office job, considering this to be more permanent and secure. My mother's family had all been in the art line, mainly as picture restorers, one or two in allied occupations such as architects, and there had now been four generations engaged in artistic pursuits. However, my uncles had sons of their own to consider and were naturally averse to encouraging their sister's offspring as competitors.

On 14th November, a Saturday, I left the office at lunchtime and went to the Adam and Eve Mews, off Kensington High Street, and entered the Drill Hall, empty except for a sergeant seated at a table in the centre. I answered the various questions, giving a fictitious age of 19, and was sent up to the gallery to await the Medical Officer, who eventually turned up, evidently from his enjoyable lunch. I took off my jacket and was told to hold out my arms, open and close my fingers; the MO said OK and turning on his heel walked off. No stethoscope was used and no pulse rate taken. I assumed I had passed this farcical medical examination and went back to the table where I was sworn in and signed on. I did not get the proverbial King's Shilling and assumed the sergeant had kept this as his 'perks'. I was told to report back on Monday morning.

I went home and broke the news, which was taken rather badly by my mother, and in silence by my father. I had joined the 3rd battalion, our 1st battalion was in France, the 2nd battalion being a home service unit was at Watford.

We in the 3rd battalion had then no uniforms or rifles, except for a few wooden dummy rifles. We drilled in Holland Park and Hyde Park, with occasional route marches and field exercises in Richmond Park or Barnes Common, going home each evening. We drew 7/- a week pay, less 4d for National Insurance, plus £1 per week subsistence allowance and travelling expenses while living at home. After a few weeks we were issued with khaki uniforms. We felt privileged to get these, as the newly formed Kitchener's Army, of which there was a Kensington Battalion, had to be satisfied with blue uniforms made from Post Office cloth. We felt very proud as we marched along High Street, Kensington singing:

We are the Kensington Boys
We are the Kensington Boys,
We spend our tanners
We mind our manners,
We are respected wherever we go,
When we're marching down the High Street Ken,
Doors and windows open wide.
You can hear the sergeant shout,
Put those blooming Woodbines out,
We are the Kensington Boys.

Our 1st Battalion, before going to France had been billeted in the stadium of the White City. A very celebrated firm of caterers had supplied their food, eventually resulting in a bad epidemic of food poisoning. Our colonel seemed to take a delight in leading the battalion past Cadby Hall, where we would march to the accompaniment of loud boos, much to the delight of the female employees who would lean from the windows, dressed in cotton overalls and caps, waving to us as we passed by.

Some of our more ribald songs were much appreciated by many of the spectators lining the kerbs, but looked on with distaste by a few of the more snobbish residents of the Royal Borough.

Another satirical song was:

We are Fred Karno's army
A scruffy lot are we.
We cannot march, we cannot fight
What blooming good are we?
And when we get to Berlin
The Kaiser he will shout,
'Mein Gott, Mein Gott, What a ruddy fine lot
Are the British Ar-Armie.'

I was also very proud to walk in the evening and at weekends with my friends along Green Lanes, Harringay. Most had now joined up, two in my battalion, one in the Navy and one artillery.

At a concert in the drill hall one night I had my first experience in getting completely blotto on neat whisky, under the tuition of a young fellow who claimed to be from Texas. He possessed a cheap and antiquated revolver and a phoney American accent to prove his story. We imbibed extremely large quantities in quick succession, ignoring the kindly warnings from the canteen sergeant's wife. I ended up feeling terribly ill and sleeping on the drill hall floor, someone covering me up with the heavy and filthy curtain from the stage. My 'Texan' friend woke me in the morning (Sunday) and escorted me to a coffee shop where I was handed a plate of fat bacon and eggs with coffee, which I found very difficult to digest, afterwards staggering to South Kensington Station and thence home. My parents and sister were sitting down to Sunday dinner, as I poked my head in the door and mumbled 'Hello – I'm going to bed.' I swore to myself that I would never partake of strong liquor again, but have to confess that this vow was soon broken. Christmas 1914 was spent at home.

Here I must recount the episode of the German spy, a hairdresser in Green Lanes, Harringay. One day I entered for a trim up, and the barber, a typical Teutonic type, started asking very pointed questions about my battalion – if we had rifles etc. Being suspicious of him I gave very misleading replies, saying we did indeed have rifles. Did they come from the Tower of London? I said I did not know. In fact the old surplus rifles were originally stored there, but had now been issued to the new army. Our battalion had no rifles at the time – the 2nd Battalion had Japanese rifles and bayonets, made by BSA in Birmingham, but confiscated by our Government on the outbreak of war.

The barber's wife, a large dark woman, peeped through the inner door and looked at me with a very scared expression, then quickly disappeared behind the scenes. I did think of reporting the incident to the police, but decided that it would most likely be a waste of time. I read after the war that he was indeed a German spy, and known to the authorities, and in common with other spies was left alone; as they were being fed with conflicting information, their reports to Germany were confusing and useless. He had a wireless set in his roof, very little being known about wireless by the general public in those days. I had two more encounters with spies when in France as I will relate later.

One morning we entrained to a place in Essex to dig trenches (part of defences against possible invasion). I learned this ditty on the train:

> I was walking with a soldier in the Park,
> I was talking to a soldier for a lark,
> When he kissed me and told me
> That he'd marry me as well,
> Then he borrowed my purse and left me
> A soldier's farewell.

I found trench digging very exhausting in the heavy wet clay and was thankful when the time came to return home. My efforts, like those of many others, were very unimpressive when compared with those of fellows used to manual work.

No one in my squad had any experience of drill, and I was appointed as squad commander for a short time, owing to having had some small training in the Lad's Brigade, although I felt a little embarrassed because of my extreme youthfulness and being at the time very immature. I had, however, bought the standard drill manuals on company and battalion drill; also my father had given me a very good book on map reading, all of which I had thoroughly digested. This small promotion however was to be very short-lived, as after Christmas a party of us were entrained to Watford and transferred to the 2nd Battalion, mostly composed of Home Service men. I had of course enlisted for overseas service, hence the reason for overstating my age. The minimum age for Home Service enlistment was 18, and for Overseas Service 19.

We were now issued with the Japanese rifles and bayonets and leather equipment, besides which we were provided with a long canvas kit-bag for our personal belongings.

The 2nd Battalion were remarkably well trained and disciplined, really up to Guards' standard, and regimental pride and esprit de corps were extremely high. Many of the men had previously been employed at local firms, such as Barkers, Pontings, Holland Hannon and Cubitts, and so on. We drilled in Cassiobury Park, and did long route marches and field exercises in the surrounding countryside.

I was billeted in a furnished bedroom with a very nice fellow (Peter Ling) a teacher by profession. We spent most our spare time together, exploring the town and sampling the local (Watford) brew in a temperate manner, the town being famous for its breweries.

After church parade on Sunday mornings the rest of the day was usually our own and several times I and another fellow, in common with others, broke bounds and dodging the regimental police, would make our way across the fields catching a train from Watford Station enabling us to get home for tea. Once the train did not stop at Tottenham Hale and we both jumped from the moving train to the platform. I fell, badly bruising my knee cap and tearing my trousers. I managed the several miles walk to get home to Harringay.

We eventually left Watford for Saffron Waldon, marching long distances for three days, stopping at Ware and Hertford in barns or billets for the nights. There was much competition between the four battalions of the Brigade, for march discipline, etc., our battalion being the winners, to the chagrin of the London Scottish who prided themselves on their marching ability; we had the smallest number of men falling out. No doubt the London Scottish were hampered in the hot weather by the weight of their kilts. The Scots were very cunning, hiding their casualties behind hedges and haystacks, but were discovered by the eagle eye of the Brigadier General.

It was at Hertford I believe where my section was lucky to be billeted in an empty room above an old inn. We spent a convivial evening in the private room of the innkeeper's family, retiring late to our bare attic above. In the night we tipped our dirty water and slops out of the window. There was a hard frost and our slops ran down the front window of the bar below, much to the annoyance of the innkeeper who discovered the state of his frozen windows in the morning.

We were pleasantly surprised when we arrived at Saffron Waldon, then a lovely old town composed mainly of mediaeval buildings and timbered houses, the entrances of many being very low, the floors often below street level. The inhabitants were mostly Quakers, who kept their daughters out of sight. We hardly saw a young girl all the time we were there.

My section were billeted in a fine, empty, large modern house on the outskirts of the town, with the company cooks installed below. We slept on bunks made of three loose planks raised on very low trestles and with straw filled mattresses. We had as usual to keep our quarters scrupulously clean, for inspection by the orderly officer each morning, and if as much as a matchstick was found on the floor we missed our breakfast. Each morning we ran a mile or so in shirt sleeves before breakfast. Some fellows would fall out, but I always managed to finish the run, although with much distress through want of breath.

One morning I woke with a violent attack of dysentery and stayed in my bunk, but was severely reprimanded by the Orderly Officer for not first attending parade to get permission to go sick. I managed to get before the Medical Officer without mishap and was given a large dose of peppermint and light duty. This entailed sitting on the guard room floor and undertaking various chores throughout the day. I was cured by evening.

One day we were sent to the firing range to try our new Japanese rifles. While waiting I entered the canteen and drank a pint of ginger beer (very gassy). On emerging I saw a crowd of London Scottish round a fellow who was brandishing a pair of boxing gloves and challenging anyone to go three rounds. No one seemed eager to oblige him, so being fond of the sport I agreed to have a go. I held my own very well for the 3 x 2 minute rounds, but the ginger beer left me so winded that I was not displeased when the bout was over. Naturally my effort on the firing range immediately after was not at all impressive, although eventually I became a first class shot.

A few days after this I ran into my opponent who congratulated me on my performance and said I had given him a few good knocks and that it was evidently not the first time I had the gloves on. I did not disillusion him by saying that my previous experiences were very limited, being mainly obtained in a Church hall with various keen companions, very rough and earnest bouts, sometimes causing much concern and distress to the vicar who would beseech us to be more gentle. It transpired that my opponent had been runner up in the ABA light-weight championships. He would thus have been about my own weight at the time, my only advantage being height. He would undoubtedly have beaten me in a serious contest. However, I was well pleased with my performance, and seemed to have impressed the spectators.

We went through very thorough training in battalion, company and arms drill, becoming very proficient and smart. Discipline was extremely severe. I once had the opportunity of watching the battalion on parade from an excellent vantage point above the field. All the movements including presenting arms, fixing bayonets, etc. were most impressive and perfect. I was a good judge of this, having seen so much of it performed by the Guards during my boyhood. I could not fault the display. As far as actual warfare was concerned, however, this kind of training was only of use in instilling immediate obedience and discipline. Apart from a few feeble lectures and field manoeuvres, more or less out-dated, we had no training applicable to trench warfare, which we had to learn later the hard way, by actual war experience.

One day we were drilled and inspected before the Brigadier General; there were about 700 or 800 of us in the ranks. At the conclusion the Brigade Major came across the field directly to me, much to my consternation, thinking that I was about to be criticised for some fault. He asked if I had ever considered promotion and advised me to do so. This gave me quite a thrill, but I did not want promotion, feeling rather immature and inexperienced, and also preferring freedom when off duty. I had noticed that our corporals seemed to have a pretty thin time, getting frequent extra work such as orderly corporal, etc., and appeared to be used as general dogsbodies. I preferred to stay as an ordinary private. However, later on when in France I sometimes had to take over responsibility as senior in service whenever an NCO was not available. This was the first of three similar contacts at Brigade level, as I will recount later.

Our 2nd battalion was very fortunate in having one of the finest brass bands in the Territorial Army, mostly composed of professional musicians from London theatres, complete with magnificent instruments. Also we had a fine drum and fife band. We were livened up with marching tunes on our route marches and Church parades, and the band was often loaned to other units in the Brigade. The most popular tune was 'The Uniform Grey', which incidentally was composed by our fierce old Colonel MacLean. I do not remember the verses, but the song started off with our Regimental Call 'Daa Daa Daa – Daa daa dada dada da Dah,' the chorus being:

Here's success to the thirteenth Grey
A regiment fine down Kensington way.
A smarter corps was never made
Than that which leads the Grey Brigade.
Westminsters, Civils, Scots and the rest,
Artists and Devils are all of the best,

Where will you find such men displayed
Except in the ranks of the Grey Brigade.
Dah, Dah, Dah.
(That's all rot).

the last words being introduced satirically in order to save our faces, the British soldier delighting to poke fun at himself, and hating to sound boastful.

We had one or two old soldiers in the battalion, very similar in type and looking well over age. They were thin, wiry men of undernourished appearance and with whitish complexions, apparently existing on copious amounts of beer of which they consumed twenty or more pints a day whenever available, neglecting solid food. They spent hours daily in cleaning their equipment, polishing and 'boning' their boots and leather belts to a miraculous brilliance. They were much given to bragging and at times inclined to be touchy and aggressive. We younger men held them in some awe, especially as they gave the impression of being dangerous men to quarrel with, having no respect for Queensberry Rules or such fine aspects as fair play. Following the theory that 'old soldiers never die' they usually managed to get onto headquarters detail as regimental police, cooks, grooms or the like. They showed great aptitude in running gambling games or 'schools', such as 'pontoon', 'housey-housey', and 'crown-and-anchor', the latter surreptitiously as it was for some reason strictly forbidden. These activities kept them well in funds and paid for their beer.

The original drum and fife band, mostly young boys, with their white haired old Drum Major Skinner, a very ancient Grenadier Guardsman, were out in France with the 1st battalion and were engaged on carrying parties, etc. when in the line. Having their drums and fifes with them when out at rest, they polished up their instruments and gave fine performances up and down the villages to the great entertainment of both ourselves and the French civilians. They also formed a concert party, one popular farce, a trench play, being written by one of the drummers. I met him again after the War, on holiday at Shanklin. He had been buried by a shell in France, dug out and sent home to a psychiatric hospital in

Scotland to recover from the dreadful shock.

Colonel MacLean was a rather aged and violently tempered old gentleman. We only saw him on battalion parades and manoeuvres – thank goodness. With his small pointed moustachios he reminded me of Mephistopheles. He was always mounted on his horse and from that vantage point would scream at us in a very shrill and terrifying manner, calling us all the foul names he could muster up. If he could find no valid excuse for this he would soon make one up. Woe-betide anyone who had the misfortune to go before him on a charge – his sentence was always severe. Probably his irascibility was due to the fact that his advanced age prohibited him from going to France, in spite of his numerous pleas. After the War the old rascal took up Holy Orders and one day the newspaper placards bore the legend in huge type 'Clergyman Assaults his Housekeeper'. I do not remember the outcome of the case.

While here we learned of the splendid feats of our 1st Battalion in France. At Neuve Chapelle they lost 160 men. The attack had broken the German lines for the first time in the war. Later at Aubers Ridge the losses were 436 men, reducing the battalion strength to 30%. As a fighting force the battalion was practically non-existent. Our battalion was the only one which managed to penetrate the German lines and gain all its objectives. Among several awards granted for the great gallantry shown in this action was a DSO to Captain (later Lieutenant-Colonel) E.G. Kimber.

Sir H. Rawlinson commanding the IV Corps met the survivors and congratulated them on their excellent work, which had not been in vain, the terrible pressure on Ypres had been relieved and the French enabled to gain the victory around Arras. He continued, and I quote from the Regimental History, *The Kensingtons:*

> By your splendid attack and dogged endurance you and your fallen comrades won imperishable glory for the 13th London Battalion. It was a feat of arms surpassed by no battalion in the Great War. Though no accounts of your work on that day have been published in the press, do not think that it is not known and fully appreciated. It is known and fully valued in the highest degree by myself and the Staff of the IV Corps, by General Sir John French and the H.Q. Staff and by the authorities at home.

Owing to the heavy losses the Brigade was pulled out of the trenches until sufficient reinforcements could be sent out from England, and was put on to Lines of Communication, which consisted mainly of railhead duties in various parts of Flanders.

My friend Peter Ling was now in another billet in Saffron Waldon, but we still met and spent our evenings and week-ends wandering about the old town and sampling the many old inns. One Saturday afternoon we walked to a village a few miles distant to visit a friend of mine at his artillery camp. This was rather a disappointing visit as my old acquaintance seemed to have little interest in us, evidently being fully employed in chasing the young girls who were hanging about the camp. However, our walk proved enjoyable, as the country scenery was very fine in this locality.

One Sunday afternoon Peter Ling and I visited Cambridge, about 20 miles distant by train, and my companion showed me some of the colleges. He had been here during his training as a teacher. The weather was perfect and we spent an enjoyable hour rowing on the river. Living in country surroundings was a great pleasure to me, as except for a week or two each year on holidays my life had been mostly confined to the built up areas of London. I particularly liked the route marches and the tactical exercises carried out in open fields and parkland, sometimes in the vicinity of Audley House.

We eventually left our comfortable billets and went under canvas in nearby pleasant parkland, where my parents paid a short visit, only an hour or so being allowed for this.

I was now anxious to get out to France, and one day volunteers were asked for a draft of 40 men. There was an immediate rush for this from we who had signed for overseas service, but the list was closed before I got my turn. This was a terrible disappointment to me, and I haunted the Orderly Room pleading with the Adjutant for a place on the draft. My opportunity came when the mother of one boy gave his real age away to the authorities and he was taken off the list, my name being accepted in his place. I was the last private to go out to France from the 2nd Battalion to the 1st, although when conscription came into force the Home Service men were indeed sent out as our 2nd Battalion. Otherwise I would have gone with them to Ireland, France, Salonika, Palestine and to the capture of Jerusalem when they drove the Turkish Army out of Palestine acquitting themselves with honour.

We on the draft were then inoculated and vaccinated, receiving the customary thirty hours' excuse from duties in order to recover from our stiff arms. Unfortunately someone starting a sparring match with me and the dressing was knocked off my vaccinated arm, which went septic. I was unable to carry on with bayonet exercise in the morning, the sergeant sending me once more to sick parade. A fresh dressing was applied and light duty prescribed. This entailed scrubbing the Orderly Room floor, bad arm or not. I thought this was about the limit and attended normal drills the next day. Needless to say I never again went sick. The army certainly did not encourage men to report to the doctor.

Having heard (erroneously) that buttons and brasses were not allowed to be polished in France, I obstinately refused to clean mine, which soon assumed a very dirty green condition. The platoon officer reprimanded me over this, but did not know if my claim had really any official backing. I was the only man in the battalion with dirty brasses, and was allowed to get away with it. I was very proud of my green buttons, but was to regret this later.

Shortly after this the draft was given the customary four days' leave before embarkation. I returned home with my kit-bag containing personal belongings, being allowed only to take regulation army equipment to France. Thus I was able to see my parents, sister, aunts and uncles before departing on the great adventure. My dear father gave me a solemn lecture on the grave dangers and temptations awaiting me from the wicked foreign women – all of which I was of course fully aware of.

Returning to camp at Saffron Waldon we were issued with the old Long Lee Enfield rifles and webbing equipment (plus the First Field Dressing fitted into a pocket under the tunic), and told to change the rifle and bayonet for the newer Short Lee Enfield as soon as we could get the opportunity to pick one up.

The draft then entrained to Victoria (or Waterloo Station – I forget which) and thence to Southampton under the wing of a young lieutenant. We were marched to a huge camp of tents on a hill outside the town, and spent the evening visiting Southampton and returning to camp by tram.

In the morning we marched off to Southampton Docks, escorted by our young lieutenant, who in some mysterious manner had got prints of our photographs which he had taken the previous day. I still have my copy of the tiny print, now rather faded. The officer then bade us farewell and we embarked on a large steamer which was so crowded with troops that it was difficult to find space to lay down on the upper deck. It was impossible to go below, the stairways being crammed with sleeping men. It was 16th August 1915.

Paree, that's the place to be,
Just across the sea from Dover.
Paree, that's the place to go,
Oh! Oh! Oh! Oh! Oh! what a show.
Dancing on the boulevard
Lots of pretty sights to see,
Over there, we've been told
Makes you feel like a two year old,
Who'll go to France with me.

Not that we ever had the luck to see Paris.

The journey over was uneventful, our ship being accompanied by a naval vessel as protection against submarine attack. We reached Le Havre next morning after a voyage of about twenty hours or so, and proceeded up the mouth of the River Seine. The estuary was very wide and flat for some miles, until the banks narrowed and hills rose up from the riverside, thickly wooded with green trees. Pretty villages were nestling amongst the trees and as we passed them the inhabitants crowded the landing-stages and quaysides waving and cheering wildly. It is good to remember that the French welcomed us with such enthusiasm in those days.

II

The Weaning Period

Arriving at Rouen, we disembarked and were marched through the town up to a camp on a hill, and allocated to tents. The country around was covered in scrub, very wild and rough. Sergeant instructors gave us a talk, mainly on the dangers laying in wait for us from the Ladies of the Streets, and the fearful results to be expected for those who consorted with them. We were then allowed out to visit the town. I and a companion made our way into Rouen, which was well populated with civilians and troops of many units. An elderly Frenchman invited us into his evidently bachelor flat for a glass of wine, much appreciated, although we were unable to converse, and soon left to look around. I remember the Joan of Arc memorial behind its iron railings. Out of curiosity we visited the Red Lamp district and entered one establishment, a large almost bare hall with red walls and some very insipid wall paintings. It was quite deserted for some reason and looked very dingy and we soon left, making our way back to camp. Incidentally throughout our visit we had constantly to shoo-off numerous little boys offering to lead us to enjoy the blandishments of their 'sisters'.

Next morning was medical inspection, the first real one I had received, including stethoscope, pulse reading, having to cough and say 99, a form filled and that was over. No comment was made about the depression in my ribs, which I was afraid might bar me from going to the front. We next had a hair-cut; I chose a short 'convict' crop, which I immediately regretted as it made me look more like a convict or German than an Englishman.

For several days we were given some war-like and blood-thirsty instruction by old army sergeants. This entailed simulated attacks over barbed wire and trenches, bayonet fighting, grenade throwing, etc.

We were then entrained in primitive looking railway carriages with plain wooden seats, packed in tightly on top of our equipment, spending hours over our journey to St Omer, which was then the BEF Army Headquarters. We passed the outskirts of Paris, and my neighbour pointed out the famous race course (I think it was called 'Chantilly') and said he had been a jockey and knew it well. The French railway stations in the larger towns were generally very imposing looking examples of architecture and much superior in appearance than our own. The country in Flanders was mainly very flat and uninteresting. There were very few hedges, the fields being divided by shallow ditches. We sometimes passed small orchards loaded with lovely ripe apples, and would have loved to be able to alight and help ourselves to a few. Penalties for looting, however, were extremely heavy and would have deterred us even if given the opportunity. Fruit was something we were hardly, if ever, to enjoy in France.

Our draft arrived at St Omer station, and we marched through cobbled streets to a large camp on the outskirts of the town. Through a gateway ran a straight road on the right of which was a high brick wall bordering the town. Waggons and limbers lined this wall. On the left was an extensive area of flat muddy ground interspersed with shallow drainage ditches and covered with groups of bell-tents, fitted with wooden floor boards, each tent accommodating 8 men. We were issued with blankets and allocated to tents. The whole of the ground was deep in mud.

There were, I suppose, about 50 or so of the 1st Battalion men in camp, many others being dispersed in various parts of Flanders on railhead duties. These were the remnants of our original force. I was at once aware of their generally quiet and serious demeanour, different from that of the yet untried fellows at home. They were, however, very conscious of the fine record they had earned for themselves, but welcomed us in a generous and friendly manner.

Much interest was displayed at the sight of my lovely green brass buttons, and I was told that it would be impossible for me to pass the guard at the gate for an evening visit into the town unless my equipment and boots were scrupulously clean and polished. I had left my button-cleaning kit in England, and one of the chaps kindly lent me his until I could buy my own in the canteen. It took me hours to get the dirt and corrosion off buttons, cap badge and buckles and obtain the necessary brilliance once more. Also it was quite a problem to traverse hundreds of yards over very deep mud and ditches without unduly fouling my boots. However, with a companion I managed to pass the sentry at the gate and proceed into the town.

The roads were cobbled with stones about the size of large oranges, and one had to step very cautiously in our thick iron-studded boots to avoid a slip-up, until used to these cobblestones. There were plenty of shops, a few very smart, especially one sports goods shop which I was surprised to see, with a beautiful display for a small provincial town. Some of the butchers had queer looking carcasses hanging outside, which I later discovered were horse meat, very popular with the thrifty French. The cafes and estaminets were interesting and so different from our own public houses, having marvellous selections of wines and other drinks which were so far unknown to me, giving a wonderful opportunity to sample the delights, the prices of which were unbelievably low. A very popular teetotal drink was the sweet and sticky Citron and also Grenadine. Nowadays of course most if not all of these beverages are available in English pubs, but at very enhanced prices.

Back in camp we settled down on the hard boards for the night. The bugler having sounded 'Lights Out' we soon heard the Sergeant Major trudging round in the mud and banging his cane furiously on the tent sides wherever there was a candle still alight. I was warned to keep my boots tucked out of sight at night, as there were one or two chaps with disgusting habits who would use their neighbour's boot rather than get up and go outside the tent in the mud. One fellow threw the contents of a boot through the tent flap and scored a hit on the Sergeant Major who was doing his nightly rounds. There was of course a terrible row over this.

A few weeks prior to my arrival, Eric Kennington, later to become a celebrated war artist was invalided home from my section, having been accidentally shot through the foot. His well known picture of the Kensingtons at Laventie, painted on glass, depicted a group of men resting in the snow after an arduous spell in the trenches. Their features are so well depicted that I recognise all of them. I regret that I missed meeting this artist.

The field kitchens were positioned alongside the road, and were kept scrupulously clean, the big iron dixies being greased and set alight, wiped off while hot and left shining like silver. Unfortunately when later on the battalion went back to the fighting area this cleanliness was not continued. The cooks, including their surly sergeant, were a filthy lazy lot on the whole. We often found nails and fag ends in the stew. At one time the tea, which often tasted of stew, was very highly scented, and it was found that the cooks used to wash and shave in water from the dixies, and in one case a cook was seen scrubbing the lice from the seams of his shirt, the dixies standing under the bench and receiving the results of the brushing. Men on light duty from sick parade would be put to work with the cookhouse chores, and we once saw a man with a shocking influenza cold, slowly stirring a dixie of boiled rice, his nose dripping into the dixie. I could never understand why more supervision was not exercised over the cooks. This was a terrible reflection on our once proud and smart battalion.

The London Rifle Brigade and the Rangers were in tents adjacent to ours. On leaving camp for our evening outings we would generally see one or two unfortunates undergoing first field punishment, being tied by wrists and ankles crosswise to wagon wheels. They would call to us to loosen their bonds a little, and if no one in authority happened to be about, we would do this for them. I understand that nowadays this form of punishment, as well as pack-drill, has been abandoned.

The battalion as I have said was now on Lines of Communication (Railhead duties), being only about 150 strong, my draft being the first out to increase its strength. The duties entailed sending an NCO and about eight or a dozen men to do temporary or more permanent jobs in different parts of Flanders. There were guards to be provided at railheads, parties for detraining guns and waggons from railway trucks, guards for prisoners both British defaulters and Germans, hospitals, escorting prisoners and so on. Many of these jobs were in more or less pleasant villages, some in St Omer itself, and were a welcome change from the front line. We knew however that when the battalion was once more at full strength a return would be made to the battle area, being replaced by other battle-worn and depleted units. Beyond one or two token parades those in camp were left much to their own devices, and many an hour was spent in exploring the town and visiting the numerous cafes and estaminets.

Some of us visited the Red Lamp to satisfy our curiosity. There was also a Green Lamp which I believe was reserved for officers. Inside was a large hall or room, with a staircase. The *madame* sat at a raised cashier's desk to collect the five or ten francs. The place was fairly full of troops, sitting around on chairs. A few girls were walking about in short filmy shifts, and occasionally would escort a client upstairs. Those descending would make their way out or join their friends, more or less sheepishly and the girl would sit on a knee here and there seeking another client. We cleared off after a minute or two, having no inclination to join in the sordid proceedings.

Very rarely a German plane would visit us and drop a small bomb to liven things up a bit. One hit the hospital sheltering German wounded. I did duty one night at the hospital, where we slept on stretchers at one end of the ward, full of German wounded. Our only job was to escort one of these men to the toilet when necessary. They were in no condition, or even so inclined as to cause trouble. This was where the bomb had fallen a few days before. We had a giant of a fellow with us who was a good German linguist. I asked him what the prisoners were talking about, but he abruptly told me to shut up. He was no doubt there to listen in to their conversation for official purposes.

About a dozen of us under a sergeant had a pleasant break at a delightful little village called Watten, about five miles away from St Omer. Our job was to detrain 18 pounder artillery guns and limbers when the train arrived each day. These guns were loaded one on each rail truck. We had to knock out the wooden wedges nailed to the floor at each wheel. The work had to be done quickly and was quite hard, using sledge hammers, and it was tricky jumping from truck to truck across the buffers – a fall between would have broken some bones. We took the opportunity of going through the carriages used by the artillery officers, searching for cigarette packets and it was surprising how many still contained a precious cigarette.

We sometimes had to unload and stack bales of hay (1 cwt each, but a few weighed 2 cwt). They came mostly from America. I had great difficulty at first in hoisting these on to my back, but soon got the knack of it. I often wondered how we managed to avoid a rupture. There is no doubt that this hard work coupled with simple food and fresh air, strengthened my rather frail frame until I became really tough and was afterwards able to withstand so much fatigue and strenuous work.

Our time at Watten was our own every day after unloading was done. We were there for over a week.

There had been no pay since coming to France, so by now we were completely broke. Two of us met a very nice French soldier who was in the French medical corps. He spoke excellent English and kindly treated us to several coffees. He also gave me a book, the *Master of Ballantrae* I think, which unfortunately my sergeant borrowed and left behind when we moved. By a strange coincidence he knew two ladies across the road from my home and said he sometimes visited them when in England. We exchanged letters once (before the Somme Battle obliterated our thoughts, but not I hope my friend's life).

Someone lent me a franc and I bought a simple fishing line, float and hook, and the two of us fished in the lovely canal running beside the tile warehouse, complete with barge where we slept and fed in the loft. I only caught one very small perch which we fried, but it was too small for even one decent bite.

One fellow had, against regulations, a pocket Kodak. He sat on the end of the barge to take our photograph and in his eagerness slipped off into the canal, soaking himself and ruining his precious camera, which however he could have been shot for possessing. The weather being very warm I tried sleeping under the stars on the barge, but not for long, as huge water rats were soon running over me.

Another fellow and I found a punt, and after an erratic start soon learned to manipulate it up and down the picturesque canal. We were eating two lovely big apples given to us by a young boy, when on the bank of a private estate appeared a very elegant lady who accosted us and in beautiful English accused us of stealing her apples, demanding them back, half eaten as they were. We refused to give them up much to her indignation.

Speaking of apples, one villager had an enormous tree in his front garden, loaded with huge red apples. He invited two of us to his house for coffee with his family, on condition that we brought some tins of bully beef – greatly appreciated by the French. We arrived with a couple of tins and departed with two apples each.

Next day we met another punt along the canal, poled by a very good looking French girl of about 20, dressed in the usual black blouse and skirt of the peasant. She pulled up at the wooden landing stage of a pretty little cottage and invited us to do likewise. Although she did not speak English we all seemed to understand one another. She was curious about our civil jobs and earnings.

A peculiar thing about the French peasants was that they imagined the English to be wealthy and that we all had servants at home. She was rather flirtatious and made a dead set at me, after deliberating between the two of us, kissing me and inviting us into the cottage where her old mother was sitting, her foot very swollen and swathed in bandages. The young brother was sent to the village for a tot of rum. This was the boy who had given us the apples. We were given coffee and rum and shown photographs of her fiancé who was away in the army. She stole one of my photographs and would not give it back, and asked me to come and sleep at the cottage that night.

That evening I got permission from the sergeant to absent myself for a few hours. It was dark and I could not find any path leading to the cottage, the fields being divided by wide ditches and marshy, and I did not feel inclined to attempt the punt in the dark, so decided to stay in the billet. I wonder what eventually happened to Rachel Hendrique. I have since read a book by a young officer named Edmund Blunden, who also spent a few days at Watten, and he describes his romantic affair with a young girl at the railway station. This seems a remarkable coincidence, as there was also another young girl who, armed with a French-English phrase book asked me to sit on the platform with her and study this together, but we both soon became bored and she wandered off.

There were several children who hung about worrying us for buttons and badges or other souvenirs, as was quite usual in these villages, but we were much shocked sometimes to hear respectable looking young girls reciting long strings of the foulest kind of English and waiting for us to laugh. I believe and hope that they did not realise what they were saying, and I felt disgusted and ashamed that there were British soldiers who would stoop to amuse themselves in this way.

There was a nice house in the village where we could be served with a coffee. One day we entered the nice clean living room and in an armchair in the centre was seated an upright and dignified young woman, tall, dark and handsome looking. She sat very still and calm. Several neighbours came in at intervals and sat silently in front of her for a while. It was much like a religious ceremony, with people coming to pay homage to the Virgin Mary, and we felt rather like interlopers. She was evidently soon to become a mother. This seemed quite a normal custom, as I afterwards saw similar instances on several other occasions.

One day I was detailed to fetch our rations from St Omer. I caught the train and walked to our HQ stores and was supplied with a huge quantity of supplies, quite impossible for one man to carry. A storeman kindly fetched a hand-cart and we pushed the load up over the cobbles to the Station and loaded it on to the train. On arrival at Watten I just managed to get the sacks out onto the platform in time, went to the billet and got someone to give me a hand. There was enough food to satisfy about ten times our number. After a few days we went back to St Omer, much to my regret. The weather had been delightful and sunny and the surroundings very picturesque.

The battle of Loos had just taken place and a large party of us were sent by rail to a destination where we took charge of about 1,000 German prisoners. We were allocated 4 men and about 30 prisoners to each cattle truck. When the Germans had been crowded into the trucks we fixed bayonets and loaded our rifles. One of my detail accidentally fired a round just missing my head. The Jerries looking down from the truck doors appeared terribly startled. They probably thought they were due to be shot, but realising what had happened seemed amazed that no disciplinary action was taken against the culprit.

We entered the truck and settled down by the door, all packed

At Brighton the day war was declared, 4th August 1914.

First uniform, November 1914

The draft en route to Watford, early in 1915. The author is in the background, marked with an arrow.

very close, and it was evident that there would be hardly room to use our rifles in the event of trouble. Then began a very slow journey to Le Havre, the train moving like a tortoise, sometimes going back for some reason, and making long stops both at and between stations, typical of the French railways during the war. The prisoners were a mixed lot and included a few artillerymen, which proved that the British must have penetrated deeply through the enemy lines. Some of the men were wounded. They all wore big Blücher boots, something like Wellingtons, and instead of woollen socks their feet were bound in strips of linen and rags. They made themselves as comfortable as possible on the floor, except for a tall and arrogant senior NCO or sergeant major probably – who stood up straight by the door during the whole journey which took about twenty hours. He did not look at us and never spoke except once to reprimand the artilleryman who was trying to explain to me how he was captured. A huge black-haired surly man, probably Bavarian, sat opposite, hardly taking his eyes from us, and glaring with hatred. It gave me a very uncomfortable feeling. The others seemed just ordinary docile types. One man groaned most of the time and kneeled head down, his back bared and covered with dozens of open sores; whether wounds or some horrible skin disease I do not know. We had to let several men out at most stops to attend the calls of nature, but they all came back docilely and none attempted to get away. We were ordered to relieve them of their pocket knives with which they grudgingly parted, although I had to stop one man I saw trying to hide his knife in his boot. There was a man who tried to insist on me taking his silver watch and chain, and seemed amazed when I refused.

At one stop we were issued with rations. Hard biscuits and cheese for us, but tins of bully-beef and loaves of bread for the prisoners, who seemed very surprised and puzzled to receive such preferential treatment. However, we managed to get hot water from the engine driver to make tea with our iron-rations (against the rules), but the prisoners had to make do with water. We had to lend the prisoners back their knives to open the bully-beef tins, as it was rarely possible to open them with the key provided. Some of the Germans made cigarettes with newspaper and coarse pipe tobacco. They had no cigarettes and I gave one of my few fags to the artilleryman who broke it in two to share with his companion – they seemed both very grateful.

The French drivers of passing engines would bombard us with large lumps of coal, and we had often to close the doors to avoid injury. One stop was at a training academy for French officer cadets (St Cyr I believe). Hundreds of young cadets stormed the train to do violence to the prisoners and we had to beat them off with our rifle butts before closing the doors.

We arrived at daybreak at Le Havre, formed the prisoners in a column of fours and marched through the town to the camp. Although so early, the streets were lined with civilians, men and women jeering and booing and we had to prevent many of them from physically attacking prisoners. The camp was in a large flat field with hundreds of bell tents, and the prisoners were herded twenty to a tent, almost impossible to squeeze them in as the tents were only intended to hold eight men. Some of the Germans protested and pointed to their wounded comrades, but we could do nothing about it, although I felt rather sorry for them. We then entrained and returned to St. Omer.

Soon after this a dozen or more of us under Sergeant Innis and a corporal were sent to the railhead at Merville, near Hazebrouck. Merville was a good sized country town with a station, a wide canal with wharves, and plenty of estaminets and shops. This was several miles behind the lines at Laventie, La Gorgue and Estaires. We were at first lodged in bell tents, the weather being very fine. After a token parade in the mornings the rest of the day was our own. We mounted guard at the railway about every other night. Otherwise we enjoyed a very pleasant and relaxing time. There were a few Indian troops in the vicinity and they would creep about in the night silently like ghosts – goodness knows for what purpose, and it is a miracle that none of them was shot as they crept across the railway lines between trucks. These trucks mainly contained coal, coke and rations for our army.

We made ourselves as comfortable as possible in the railway shed, sometimes sleeping on the nobbly sacks of loaves, much I fear to the detriment of the contents. One man would patrol the trucks, two hours on and four hours off. We were sometimes in a merry state after a convivial evening on bottles of cheap but potent white wine. The French must have been used to seeing the guard often staggering along the road with fixed bayonets. One very cold night we had a red hot coke brazier in the yard. This fire was foolishly placed in a bay made from bales of hay. I sat down for a rest at the brazier and fell on it, knocking it over, but doing no damage to myself or the hay. This soon sobered me up.

Another time a train which used to stop at Merville every night was fired on by an intoxicated sentry, the bullet piercing the engine and scaring the driver so much that for nights afterwards he drove through Merville at top speed without stopping at the station, until he got to Hazebrouck.

The Indians would sometimes play football in bare feet and would give us some of their very strong black cheroots. Once or twice we disturbed one creeping about in our tents. We believed they were searching for rum, which we did not possess, but we never found anything missing.

My friends were Billy Hewitt (almost a teetotaller) and Arthur Budge, both several years my seniors. Budge had been a professional teacher of tennis, and could speak French perfectly, having taught tennis in France. Billy Hewitt was a quiet chap who had owned a draper's shop in partnership with his brother, Corporal Hewitt, a cheery and well educated chap, greatly respected by the old hands for his heroism at Aubers Ridge. They all said he should have received the VC, but as far as I know he had not been given any decoration. He later left the battalion to take up a commission in another regiment. A man receiving a commission seldom came back to his old regiment – I suppose for reasons of discipline.

We were soon to be billeted in houses. Billy Hewitt and I were lucky, being ensconced in a cottage occupied by a dear old lady and her young grand-daughter (a schoolgirl – very shy). Billy and I shared a large double bed with straw mattress and canopy up in the loft of the house. The top of the canopy was an inch deep in old rat droppings, which we decided not to disturb. In the mornings the old lady would call out '*Là bas*' and we would go down and sit in her warm kitchen and be given a coffee. She was a dear old soul, and my mother sent her out a packet of handkerchiefs which she treated as a great treasure and would bring them out proudly to display to her visitors. One of these women was terribly voluble, rattling off Flemish patois at a terrific rate. When she left the old lady would say in a deprecating tone *'Flammande'*. The French peasants often seemed to despise the Flemish as of an inferior breed to themselves. We could not converse either with the grandma or grand-daughter, as they never were able to understand our attempts either at French or pigeon-french. I think that mentally they were very simple and probably only used a sort of patois dialect.

The dear old lady on discovering that we had joined the war of our own free will, found this to be incredible and astounding. She would frequently repeat the words '*Vous* volunteer!' in amazement. We found this attitude quite common with the French peasants. I suppose this was only to be expected in a country where conscription prevailed, and the compulsory national service was something to be dreaded and avoided if possible. The youthfulness of so many of the British troops was also a matter of surprise and comment. I do not think they realized that our sense of patriotism went deeper than the purely emotional.

The little girl worked very hard at her homework from school, seated at the table in the living room window. The centre of the room was occupied by the usual large round iron stove, the smoke pipe going up and out of one wall. The coffee pot, as in most of these peasant houses, was always kept hot on the stove, a little home ground coffee being added from time to time. The meals were mainly of a boiled egg, bread and butter, and vegetable soup (Julienne). I never saw meat being eaten by the peasants. Coffee was taken black, with a brandy-ball or peppermint bullseye in lieu of sugar. Whenever sugar appeared on the table, it contained a sprinkling of tea leaves, and had undoubtedly been obtained on the black market from British Army iron rations. The place was kept scrupulously clean by the old lady who seemed to spend most of her time pottering about at the sink. There was a small garden with a toilet at the back. Across the road was a large flat field divided off into allotments, full of vegetables, each allotment being bordered by a shallow ditch.

The Grenadier Guards came for a short while to an adjacent village called Paradis, and my cousin Sergeant Frankie Jones made a surprise visit to me, and insisted being taken to see the farm where we had our meals. Our sergeant and corporal were billeted here and left us pretty much to our own devices.

The Railhead Transport Officer lived in a railway carriage near the station, his office being in another carriage, complete with orderly and telephone. One day the orderly asked me to mind the telephone for an hour or so while he was absent, telling me to report by phone to a certain address if I received a call or spotted a Zeppelin, which were then passing over occasionally on their way to bomb London. One *did* pass over and I phoned the position and direction as instructed. I thought this very exciting and important, but my enthusiasm was rather damped by the casual and apparently disinterested way in which my message was received.

There were two estaminets outside the station, the less imposing one being near our cottage. This was run by two sisters, of whom more anon. We would try out our linguistic efforts with them and they were quite friendly and jolly young women. A young railway porter was keen on one of the girls, and wishing to show off, he entered one day and ordered a glass of stout, which was usually only drunk by the British, not suiting the palate of the French. With a swagger he took a gulp at the stout, and immediately ejected it with a grimace of disgust, and retired sheepishly to the station, his ardour and arrogance evidently dampened for the time being.

Billy, Budge and I had our photograph taken in the town by the local photographer. The result, which I still have, made us look rather drawn and woe-begone, although we were happy enough at the time.

We sometimes visited an estaminet in the town. This was run by two fair-haired sisters whom I thought looked more German than French. They were both very austere and reserved and it was impossible to try and get into conversation with them. I used to enjoy the glass of Malaga wine and the Dutch cigar, both only costing a copper or two. We also took several walks to La Gorgue and Estaires, a few miles distant, but fairly near the line, which was quiet at the time. In fact the artillery were so short of ammunition at that period that only one round a day was allowed to be fired from each gun.

On two occasions a prisoner had to be escorted to St Omer by train. Once a German and once an English prisoner. For some reason our corporal chose me each time to accompany him (probably because of my height). Neither gave any trouble and we marched them through the streets and handed them over to the appropriate prisons at both of which I had previously done guard duties when in St Omer camp. I was told that on a former occasion a corporal and private had got off the train at Hazebrouck and taken their German for a drink at the adjacent estaminet, the German making a getaway. Enemy prisoners were usually quite docile – happy no doubt to be out of the danger zone. The British prisoners were a much different proposition and had to be watched carefully, being defaulters and many with bad or criminal tendencies.

While at St Omer I took the opportunity to call on our QM stores to try for a new pair of boots, my own being worn right through at the soles, in spite of originally being fitted with iron studs. I was in fact walking on my bare feet, with cardboard in the soles. Supplies were very scarce at the time and my request was refused. I managed afterwards to bribe a storeman at a Guards depot with 5 francs for a good second hand pair, no doubt from a casualty. These were enormous, size 12, and raised many a blister on my heels until I was able to get a replacement months afterwards.

I was standing by the roadside one day when a small open car stopped and a man dressed as an air force officer, ginger haired, but not wearing a cap (which was unusual for an officer), asked me if I could tell him how to get to the airfield. There were a few planes in a field a mile or so away, but for some reason I was suspicious of him and said I did not know, and he drove off. I learned afterwards that there was indeed a German spy, red headed, who posed as an air force officer and drove about getting information on our planes and airfields – he went by the name of Major Samson.

Corporal Hewitt turned up one day and took Billy, Budge and myself to tea with a nice middle class French family a mile or so away. They greeted us with a fine meal and a pleasant afternoon, Corporal Hewitt acting as interpreter. The elder daughter, a very good looking and well mannered girl of about 17 or 18 rather intrigued me. A few days later Hewitt told me that they had enquired after me, calling me '*Le grand soldat dix-huit ans*'.

Sometimes units of the Indian army would pass by, mostly Sikhs and Punjabis. They were tall taciturn fellows, and some would light a small wood fire to sit around during their ten minute halt. These chaps were always complaining, and said they had to sleep in pigsties while we slept in tents. Soon I myself was only too pleased to take shelter in a pigsty. As a matter of fact, a platoon of Ghurkas were ensconced in pigsties nearby. These were happy and friendly little men, always laughing, and would willingly let us handle their *khukri* knives, without the obligation of drawing blood as was commonly supposed. There were tales of them creeping up to the enemy lines at night, and killing a German with their *khukri*, and cutting off their ears, which they prized as souvenirs.

The Sikhs and Punjabis would march to the tune of their pipes, a kind of small version of the Scottish bag-pipe. It is said that they would set up an awful lot of howling and wailing if wounded. The Indian cavalry were very smart and efficient units, and of course the Ghurkas were particularly renowned for their dash and bravery.

We noticed that the Indians did not have meat rations, but had their own live goats, which they would butcher themselves. Also they would not touch lime-juice which was sometimes issued to us, as they believed it interfered with their virility.

In November a fat little sergeant, an old army type, was billeted in the neat little bedroom downstairs. He was in fact a quarter master sergeant in the artillery and in charge of stores, evidently paying well for his comfortable abode. This chap was always half intoxicated and had ample supplies of army rum. He was so drunk one night that I took off his boots and helped him to bed. The little girl cried a lot at this time, either being scared of him or hearing that Billy and I were leaving to join the other chaps in their bare attic at another house – no doubt for reasons of economy. The old lady was very upset believing that we had asked to leave, and we could not convince her that the decision had been made by the Railhead Transport Officer. I was to see her again a year later, but not so Billy Hewitt who was wounded (through the lung in exactly the way as I was to be), nor Arthur Budge, killed at Hebuterne.

Our new quarters were not so comfortable as those we had left, and we slept on the wooden floor instead of a comfortable bed. The house owner was a little fellow (a miner) with only one arm, and we nicknamed him 'Nelson'. We would come down into the living room and amuse the family (wife and two little girls) with our antics. I would dance about on bended knees, cossack fashion, pulling awful faces, and the girls would shriek with laughter saying '*Vous comique*'.

About six of us were detailed one day to unload a barge of hay at a place just outside Merville and adjacent to an estaminet which if I remember rightly was called 'le Paquet Bot', or 'Le Grand Paquet', I forget which. There was a 9 inch plank, very muddy and slippery, from barge to bank. It was jolly hard work humping the hundredweight bales across this plank, which jumped in the middle like a yo-yo. It is surprising that none of us ended up in the canal. After finishing we entered the estaminet for a drink, and in there was the huge man whom I have before mentioned as such a good German linguist. His favourite occupation was to down as many beers in one gulp as onlookers would pay for, and we lined up half-a-dozen glasses full, which he consumed without effort. He soon left the battalion, no doubt going on a special security job, either as a spy or an interpreter.

Our letters home had to be censored by one of the junior officers. This was done in a most ridiculous manner, a perfectly innocent word being haphazardly blue pencilled for no apparent reason. Another idiotic practice was to carefully scratch out the name of a village or town printed on the picture postcards of local views; these were most certainly known to the enemy as thousands of them were sold in the local shops. About once a month we were issued with a 'green envelope', not subject to censorship, but we had to declare that nothing but strictly personal correspondence was contained therein. Dire penalties were threatened for infringement of this rule. No diaries were to be kept and no cameras were allowed under penalty of death. I have, however, known these orders to be disobeyed, especially by officers, many of whom openly quoted passages from their diaries when writing for publication after the war.

Among the new drafts from England were a number of our

second battalion (home service) men, who had volunteered for France now that conscription was in the offing. There was some resentment felt by our 'veterans' on finding that among these new arrivals were officers and non-coms who were allowed to keep their rank, thereby holding back promotion of our more experienced members. It is curious that many of us suffered from the old-fashioned prejudice regarding officers who were not drawn from the upper echelon of society or without public school education. I remember one young subaltern, a former bank clerk with a slight cockney accent, who was looked down on by the lower ranks – a case of inverted snobbery? This absurd attitude was not adopted during the Second World War, when officers were mainly chosen for their power of leadership, efficiency and intelligence, which was as well, as the men watch their officers closely for any sign of weakness, inefficiency or indecision. Lack of confidence in one's leader can have disastrous effects on morale.

The winter now set in with a vengeance and we had a good deal of snow and ice. With the help of others I filched a sack of coke from the train and staggered to my old billet, but the old lady did not show any appreciation, saying it was no good for her stove and that she preferred coal. I was found out and taken before the officer, who however said, 'If you do it again don't let me see you.'

On Christmas Eve 1915 a dozen of us were sent to the station at Estaires to clear away the heavy snowfall from the railway yard We slept in a cattle truck, it being bitterly cold, and spent the afternoon and Christmas morning working very hard to make a clearance. In the evening we went to the estaminet outside the station and sat at a long table, each drinking about twenty or more glasses of the weak French beer, but with no more effect than if it had been water. After a sing-song we went back to our truck and next day returned to Merville. I do not remember having anything special in the way of a Christmas feast.

Soon after this a contingent of Scottish Highlanders arrived to take over our jobs and billets. The inhabitants were horrified and disgusted at these men in kilts and at first refused to let them into their houses, saying '*C'est pas propre*'. They were finally appeased by the officers and we left for the camp at St Omer.

Of the twenty or so of the fellows with me at Merville, I can only call to mind the names of nine of us. It is significant of the high rate of casualties in the days to come to recall that of these nine, every one was to be killed or seriously wounded before the war was over.

The brigade had now received large reinforcements from home, and having reached full strength was destined to go into training for the fighting line. It was early in February 1916, and our reformed Brigade (168th) was comprised of the 4th Londons (Fusiliers), 12th London (Rangers), 13th London (Kensington) and 14th London (London Scottish), namely the 168th Brigade of the 56th London Division. The artillery were also Londoners, besides which we had a pioneer battalion, the 5th Cheshires.

The newly formed brigade entrained for Pont Remy and from there we marched in pouring rain to Citerne, a village surrounded by undulating country thinly populated by peasantry. The weather was very cold with heavy snowfalls. We now commenced serious training for warfare, practising modern methods of attack, weapon training including the new Lewis gun, grenade priming and throwing, use of the new gas masks, and so on. Another move was made, entailing a march of about 25 miles in snow 18″ thick, with equipment weighing over 60lbs. strapped to our shoulders. This proved very exhausting and a number of men fell out on the way. Our transport's mascot, a sturdy black retriever named 'Nigger', accompanied the battalion, running in the snow from front to rear of the column, apparently with no effort. He must have covered a hundred miles or so backwards and forwards. Much of our horse driven transport was stuck on the hills and did not arrive until a day later.

I was utterly exhausted when we arrived at our destination, a large farm near Longpré, and as we came to a halt, felt myself swaying on my badly blistered feet. Our section entered a large and leaky barn and no sooner sank down thankfully into the straw when the sergeant entered and detailed those nearest him for guard duty. I was very fortunate in being posted as the first sentry, two hours on and four off. No blankets or food arrived until the next day, when it was planned for us to move off. However as the roads were so congested with French troops and waggons on their way to the raging battle at Verdun, we were able to get a few days' comparative rest, interspersed with periods of training.

We then marched another 16 miles to Doullens. There we enjoyed a couple of days' rest and were able to explore the attractive town. After this we marched to Magnicourt, getting a demonstration of the German *flammenwerfer* or flame thrower, crouching in a trench while the terrifying weapon was jetted over us, the container and apparatus being strapped on the operator's back. We then moved to the village of Lignereuil, of which we were going to see a good deal. This was a collection of rather primitive dwellings and barns, some brick and some mud and plaster or clay. The barns were terribly infested with rats, the floors being covered in old and very filthy straw, containing old tins, buttons, cartridges, fag-ends and packets and goodness knows what else – common to all barns behind the lines. The rats were very bold. As soon as lights out they jumped by the hundred from the roof and holes in the wall with loud squeaks and thuds, quarrelling and fighting each other. They ran all over us and got into our haversacks searching for food. We had to keep kicking them off our blankets when they would drop to the hard-packed straw with a bump. One or two of the men were nibbled on the nose or ear.

Here also I was first infested with large lice. I had been immune from them up till now, but was never after free from them except when on leave and until I entered hospital towards the end of the War. We used to search our clothes and have competitions over the number caught and killed on thumbnails with a loud crack. Sometimes we would run a lighted candle down the seams of our clothes to destroy them and their eggs. We would often kill about 40 or 50 at a sitting, but still they thrived. The irritation was terrible and we could hear each other scratching wildly at our skins in the night. One favourite place for them was around our knees, a difficult place to get at them, being just above the tops of our puttees. This and the fact of being unable to wash our bodies or change our clothes for very long periods caused many fellows to get scabies, a very unpleasant affliction. Peculiarly head pests and fleas were unknown.

There were also other unpleasant skin afflictions and boils, probably due to overmuch bully-beef and lack of green vegetables and fruit. When we *did* manage to get laundered shirts and socks they were often full of someone else's dead insects, and so badly shrunk they would not fit. My socks were often Lilliputian, the heels under my instep, which made marching a torture, with huge broken blisters on my heels. We had always to keep properly shaved and our buttons and buckles brightly polished, clothes, weapons and equipment as clean and smart as possible – in and out of the line under all conditions, although in muddy trenches we were covered from head to foot in thick clay or chalk, which made things impossible. Our chief trouble was in keeping our rifles clean and free from clay.

We were soon to get steel helmets to add to our discomfort, but were grateful for them when under fire. They were more efficient than their German equivalent against rifle and shrapnel fire. We had now a new weapon in the Stokes gun, a very useful trench mortar.

In April we moved to Dainville, near Arras, under observation from enemy sausage balloons. Movement and rations had to go up at nightfall. Here we were engaged in digging reserve trenches under the direction of the Royal Engineers at night. This was very hard work in the heavy and sticky clay and chalk. After a fortnight of this we thankfully marched back to Lignereuil.

Here we held Brigade sports, the Kensingtons winning the parade and limber turnouts and the driving competitions. Someone had the brilliant idea of painting the edges of the horseshoes with aluminium paint. Naturally owing to my skill with a brush I was given this rather hazardous job. With little time to spare I managed the task, fortunately without mishap from the horses' hooves to either myself or the paint pot. No sooner was I finished than it was found that the device would be disallowed, and frantic efforts were made to obliterate my work with tufts of grass and earth – not entirely successful, but nevertheless sufficient to allow our team to win the competition. We also carried out an exercise attack using a smoke screen. We then moved to Souastre, near the Hebuterne front. More training and some football matches, beating the London Scottish and drawing with the Rangers. We also had an exercise in field sketching the view being over a valley and on to villages, churches, bridges, etc. I did a very creditable drawing, gauging distances and marking such details on the sketch. The Brigadier General came by to inspect the results and seemed much impressed by my efforts, suggesting that I should apply to be transferred to the Field Survey detachment. I did not follow his advice as I wished to remain with a fighting unit. I do not remember exactly where this exercise was carried out.

Also at a parade before the Brigadier, the Brigade Major approached me and asked why I did not put in for promotion. I preferred to remain an ordinary private in the ranks, for reasons as stated on the previous and similar occasion when in England. I was more self-confident and ambitious later in life when in the Home Guard, going through all ranks to become a first lieutenant and platoon commander.

Since leaving Merville I had been parted from my old friends and had not as yet made any new ones in my present section. There came a night as we got nearer to the line, when we were billeted in a barn, and I suddenly felt very lonely and for the first and only time a dreadful fear and home-sickness. It was a horrible feeling, but I got over this by morning. I think it was a turning point in my life – I had changed from a boy to a man.

One day I was detailed to join the Regimental police. Whether this was because of my height, or that my real age had been given away by someone at home, or an adverse medical report arrived from Rouen, I do not know. However, I had to obey orders, and spent a few weeks with about eight others under a very nasty-natured and aggressive little police sergeant. I did not like the job, especially standing about with belt and bayonet, bossing others about and ordering 'Time' at the various estaminets. Two of us were of like mind and decided to ask the Regimental Sergeant Major to let us rejoin our companies, to which he agreed. Incidentally when we arrived in the battle area, the bullying little fire-eater of a sergeant got the wind-up so badly that he was sent home with a mental breakdown. I ran into him soon after the war ended. He was serving meekly behind the counter of a stationer's shop in London.

While at Souastre I was detailed to the battalion transport section, as a brakesman. Although I know nothing about horses, I was soon put in charge of a packhorse – a lovely creature – chestnut colour and probably a hunting horse. His name was Jack. I learned to like this work very much and soon was able to ride quite well –

bareback of course, with no saddle or stirrups. We would rise at dawn and ride several miles to water, then return and feed hay before getting our own breakfasts, after which we groomed our charges thoroughly. After dinner we had to clean harness (very boring), feed corn and take turns at night picket. There was very little time to ourselves.

My first attempts at riding bare back must have been amusing, as I would slip sideways and end up hanging on under the horse's neck – very like John Gilpin. However, when I became more proficient I was delighted with riding, feeling like a king, especially when passing through a village or riding down a steep bank, leaning back cowboy fashion to keep perfect balance. At one place we had to ride a very long distance to get to water, and the weather being very wet, we all developed huge blisters on the cheeks of our posteriors, which turned into very nasty raw wounds, making further trips exceedingly painful until healed up.

Mine was one of eight pack-horses, including two mules. The small one was very playful, and led the other chaps a devil of a dance, getting the back of their shirts in his teeth and trying to lift them when being groomed, or seizing the reins in his teeth and playing tug-of-war just like a dog. Peculiarly he seemed to like me and behaved as good as gold when I was handling or riding him.

On my first night we had to sleep in a stable with the horses, and I woke to find that one had got loose and was standing right over me. I did not dare to move in the dark in case he got startled and did me some damage. Fortunately one of the chaps woke and lit a candle, and managed to get him secured again. We had one or two horses wounded by shrapnel, and they had to be treated by the vet. Most of the other horses were heavy draught animals, used for the wagon and limbers, field cookers and water wagon. There were forty horses in all, and I got to know the names of all of them. The draught horses were generally in pairs, one of each sex, and were named Jack and Jill, Adam and Eve and so on.

On one long route march my horse's pack, a large heavy box of ammunition hung from each side of the pack saddle, must have got loose. The horse suddenly turned and bolted towards the rear of the column while I, with my heavy pack and rifle to carry, was unable to restrain him, but managed to keep hold of the reins. We rushed past the Brigadier General who yelled 'Stop that horse'. He eventually stopped by a haystack which he had no doubt noticed in passing and thought he would like a feed. The ammunition boxes had by then slipped under his belly. The corporal soon arrived and we got the pack securely in position. I had to hurry a very long way to catch up with our moving section.

At one village our wagons were parked in the large courtyard of a farm, where the transport officer, then Captain Holland, was billeted in a room opening onto the yard. The drivers would converse in loud voices and every few words were accompanied by a very coarse and obscene four letter expression. One day Captain Holland came out and told the drivers to modify their language, saying, 'If you want to have an affair then have one, but don't keep talking about it.'

'Hookey' Holland was a big, rather handsome man with a very pronounced Roman nose and a reputation of having served with the Mexican army. For some reason he was greatly disliked by our drivers. One night he visited our sleeping quarters after 'lights out'. As he left there was a chorus of shouts, calling out a rather filthy insult. He turned to the sergeant and asked what the words were, and the sergeant tactfully replied '*Git back*, I think, Sir'. It certainly rhymed with that.

Once when I was engaged on a lonely night picket on the horse lines, I left my post for a minute or two to cadge a cup of tea at midnight from our adjacent cook-house. As luck would have it 'Hookey' chose this moment to ride up on his charger to make a rare visit to the lines. Entering the cook-house he asked why there was no picket on duty, and I replied that I had slipped into the cook-house for a moment to accept a 'sup' of tea, and I had to explain that the word 'sup' was intended for 'sip'. He did not reprimand me but said that a horse was loose. I think he had deliberately set it free and I spent a strenuous half-hour trying to catch the animal. At another time several of us were trying to clean wagons at a slimy stinking pond. We sat down for a smoke and rest when 'Hookey' Holland came in sight, whereupon we all jumped up and looked busy. We had, however, been seen and received a severe reprimand for being deceitful, and told that if we wanted a rest to take one and not to be dishonest about it. Why he was so disliked I do not know – personally I thought he treated us quite fairly. He was soon to be transferred to Brigade transport and was superseded by Captain Prynne, a nice gentlemanly young officer, the son of a clergyman we were told.

The battalion took over positions in the firing line at Hebuterne, opposite Gommecourt which was held by the Germans. We had to take turns to go up to the village every evening, a distance of several miles from Souastre, with wagons and limbers full of rations and ammunition, water, etc. The road up was open to flat country on both sides, and all the way we could see the flashes of the guns and shells, shrapnel bursts in the sky, and occasional Very lights and red and green signal rockets, both British and German. Often the main road in Hebuterne parallel with the trenches, was raked with long range machine gun bullets, zipping past like bees, with an occasional ricochet 'Trr, Trr, Trr', and thuds as they struck the trees and walls.

Once I rode on top of the GS Wagon which was piled high with rations, and felt very uncomfortable and exposed to the fusillade, which fortunately did us no harm. On the way back I sat on the high seat next to the driver, when the wheels went into a shell hole and the driver was pitched out into a ditch. Fortunately he was unhurt and we managed to free the wagon and get back to Souastre. It was not unusual for a driver to be pitched out into a ditch on a dark night. The drivers of the limbers of course were seated on horseback.

A young driver managed to borrow a set of boxing gloves and strutted about with a challenge, but as none of the others would have a go, I did a couple of rounds and made rings round him, to the enjoyment of the spectators, thus earning a good deal of respect for the future. Afterwards, however, I sparred with a stocky fellow, a former brewer's drayman, about three stones heavier than me, and soon found I did not stand a chance against his powerful punching ability.

Opportunity came to paint our wagons and limbers, and I volunteered to paint the divisional sign, a dagger and the words B3 on the sides, as well as one or two other signs, and obtained a reputation as a signwriter which was to come in useful later on.

Several of the brakesmen were now made redundant and sent

back to their companies. I felt sorry for one very young and simple country fellow, and asked if I could go back in his place, but my request was ignored. This boy was killed a few weeks later.

The transport officer took a fancy to my lovely horse 'Jack' and commandeered him for his own mount. I was very disappointed to have to part with him, but was given another, darker, but equally good.

Soon there was great activity in the fields behind Hebuterne – great gun pits were dug and the number of artillery guns increased, so we knew that something big was about to commence.

For a week or two before the assault our machine gunners, positioned in the rear of the trenches, would amuse themselves and us at odd times by tapping out a ditty on their gun. By skilful manipulation of their thumb on the trigger they would fire several rounds of tat-tats, emulating 'Bom-tiddy-Bom-Bom – Bom-Bom'. The German machine gunners, probably a mile or so away, would reply in like manner, but always ending with an extra 'tat'.

The enemy lines in front of Gommecourt were about 700 yards distant from ours. One night 3,000 men were sent over in the dark and dug an advanced trench (known as an assault trench) about 300 yards from the enemy lines. This was done under cover of a huge barrage of shell-fire, which made it virtually impossible for the Germans to see what was going on. This operation was performed without a single loss. I was up in Hebuterne that night with the GS Wagon. The whole place was lit up brilliantly by the light of the bursting shells, and the thunderous din was amazing and awe-inspiring. How the driver managed to control his horses I do not know, and I was glad when we were able to get back to Souastre. The next night another party went out to deepen the trench, and only a few casualties occurred.

The transport were now living in the open, the horses tethered to a long rope line or lines in a large green field. We were ensconced in shacks made from oddments of timber and corrugated iron or pieces of tarpaulin. The weather on the whole was sunny and warm, with occasionally wet periods.

I liked this sort of existence and was in my element working amongst horses – so very different to the prison-like life of a city office, which I hated.

Sergeant, sergeant, give back my stirrups to me-ee-ee,
Sergeant, sergeant, give back my stirrups to me.
I've been in the saddle an hour,
I've stuck it as long as I could,
I'm not going to stick it much longer,
My backside is *not* made of wood.
You have to be cruel to be kind.

We had one lanky fellow who suffered from some form of sleeping sickness. He would sometimes fall asleep standing up, while grooming his horse, and had to be woken up. We had a very nice young captain, a sergeant, two corporals who had some sort of bitter feud between them, a farrier, a wheelwright, a saddler and a cook.

III

Grim Reality

We learned that an assault was about to be made on Gommecourt. A detachment of men, about 100, was to remain behind in camp, as a nucleus in case the battalion were annihilated. The night before the attack we took most of the limbers, GS wagon and pack ponies up to Hebuterne, loaded with supplies, ammunition, hand grenades, picks, spades, axes, etc., and food and water. The supplies were unloaded in the main road and some of us had to carry boxes of ammunition down a lane leading to the front line and dump them in a ruined brick shed. A fusillade of machine gun fire was being directed at the spot where we approached the shed, the bullets zipping past, and causing a few casualties as we darted across the lane. I was glad when the job was finished – fortunately the enemy was not aware of what was going on, or we would have been shelled.

Next morning, 1st July 1916, the Somme battle commenced. Our division was on the left or northern part of the attack. The London Scottish went over first (that is of the Brigade), and got into the German front line, behind a terrific barrage of shell-fire. The Jerries however were well prepared and emerged from their dugouts in the support lines to resist further progress, the enemy shell and machine gun fire being terrible in intensity. The Kensingtons were in support, and endeavoured again and again to reach the Scottish, only one small party managing to get through. Valiant efforts were made to reach the Scottish with fresh supplies of rifle ammunition and grenades, the Scottish running out of supplies. Except for a few the Kensingtons were mown down trying to cross the old no-man's land. The attack on the left was really

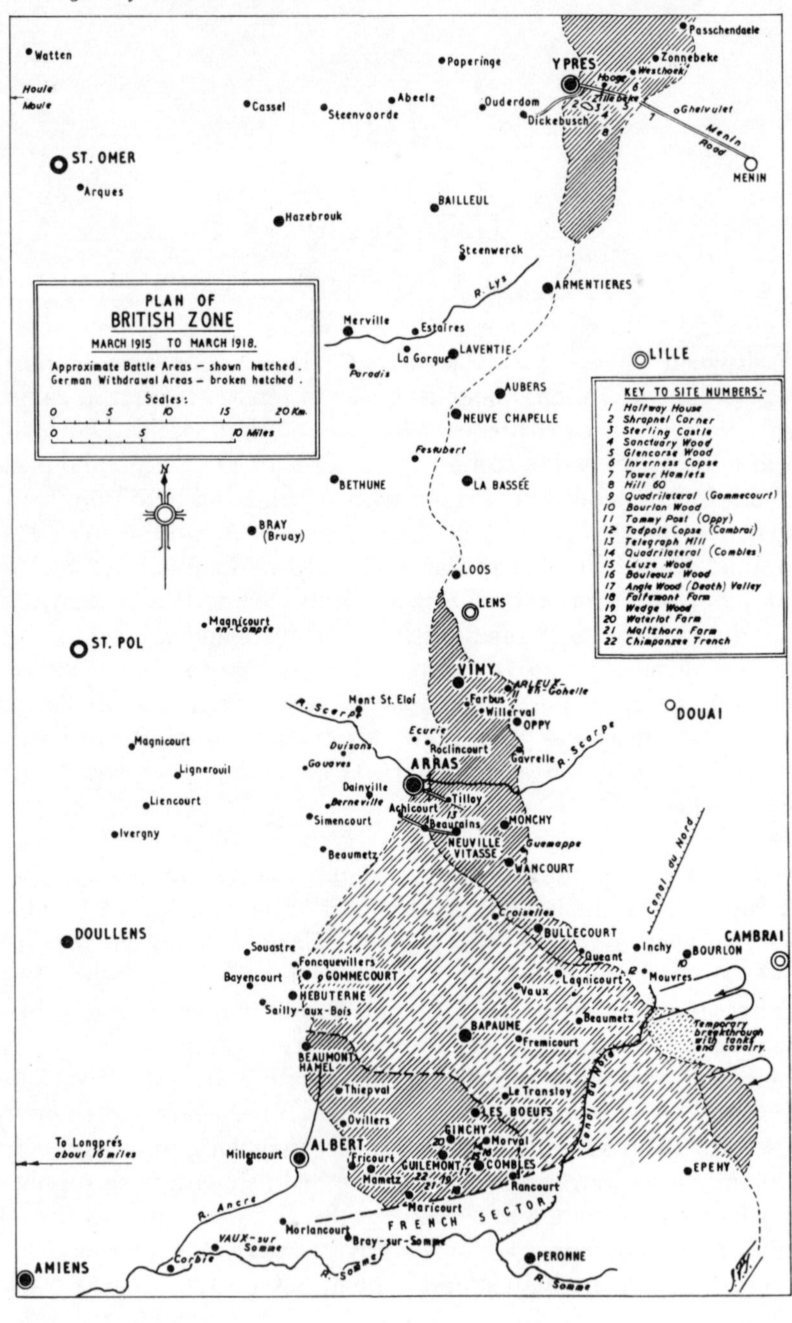
PLAN OF
BRITISH ZONE
MARCH 1915 TO MARCH 1918.
Approximate Battle Areas – shown hatched.
German Withdrawal Areas – broken hatched.
Scales:
KEY TO SITE NUMBERS:-
1 Halfway House
2 Shrapnel Corner
3 Sterling Castle
4 Sanctuary Wood
5 Glencorse Wood
6 Inverness Copse
7 Tower Hamlets
8 Hill 60
9 Quadrilateral (Gommecourt)
10 Bourlon Wood
11 Tommy Post (Oppy)
12 Tadpole Copse (Cambrai)
13 Telegraph Hill
14 Quadrilateral (Combles)
15 Leuze Wood
16 Bouleaux Wood
17 Angle Wood (Death) Valley
18 Falfemont Farm
19 Wedge Wood
20 Waterlot Farm
21 Maltzhorn Farm
22 Chimpanzee Trench
YPRES
Passchendaele
Zonnebeke
Poperinge
Watten
Cassel
Steenvoorde
Abeele
Ouderdom
Dickebusch
Ghelvulet
Menin Road
MENIN
ST. OMER
Arques
Hazebrouk
BAILLEUL
Steenwerck
ARMENTIERES
R. Lys
Merville
Estaires
LAVENTIE
La Gorgue
Paradis
LILLE
AUBERS
NEUVE CHAPELLE
Festubert
BETHUNE
LA BASSÉE
BRAY (Bruay)
LOOS
LENS
ST. POL
VÎMY
Farbus
Willerval
OPPY
DOUAI
Mont St. Eloí
R. Scarpe
Ecurie
Roclincourt
Gavrelle
ARRAS
Magnicourt
Lignerouil
Liencourt
Ivergny
Gouvres
Dainville
Berneville
Tilloy
Achicourt
Simencourt
Beaurains
MONCHY
NEUVILLE VITASSE
Guemappe
Beaumetz
WANCOURT
Canal du Nord
Croiselles
BULLECOURT
DOULLENS
Souastre
Foncquevillers
GOMMECOURT
Bayencourt
HEBUTERNE
Sailly-aux-Bois
Queant
Inchy
BOURLON
CAMBRAI
Lagnicourt
Mouvres
Vaux
Beaumetz
BAPAUME
Fremicourt
Temporary breakthrough with tanks and cavalry.
BEAUMONT HAMEL
Thiepval
Le Transloy
LES BOEUFS
Ovillers
GINCHY
Morval
To Longprés about 16 miles
Millencourt
ALBERT
Fricourt
GUILLEMONT
COMBLES
Mametz
Rancourt
EPEHY
Maricourt
FRENCH SECTOR
R. Ancre
Morlancourt
VAUX-sur Somme
Bray-sur-Somme
Corbie
R. Somme
PERONNE
AMIENS

designed to take some of the pressure off the main attack further south. Some of the companies, 150 strong, came out with only 20 men. The Kensingtons' fighting strength of 600 was reduced to 300, thus losing half its strength, the brigade having to fall back to its original positions. The enemy opposite were Saxons, who were generally considered the most decent of the bunch. Our stretcher bearers and others were out in no-man's land collecting the wounded and without molestation from the enemy. Some of the Saxons even brought wounded men up to our trenches for us to collect. The 8th Division had also attacked to the north but with no better success. All was now more or less back to normal, except that we had to stand-to for two hours each morning instead of the usual one hour, in case of a counter attack, which fortunately did not materialize, owing no doubt to the terrible battering the Germans must also have endured.

The old trenches, some being the old French front line, were now so smashed by shell-fire to be almost unrecognisable, and deep with mud.

Our old Regimental Quarter Master, Captain Ridley, a South African War veteran, broke down and wept over the losses sustained by our fine battalion of which he was so proud.

I forgot to tell of a rather amusing incident that occurred during one of our first nights in the Hebuterne trenches. A young fellow went to the latrine bay and left his rifle against the side of the pit, when suddenly two Germans who had crept up unobserved, crawled over the parapet and stole the rifle, decamping rapidly without attacking its owner. I expect they were sent over for the purpose of finding whether we were armed with the Japanese rifle used by us in England. The poor young chap was scared out of his wits. I passed him the next day and he was still in a state of shock, staring ahead with a glazed expression as though he had seen a ghost.

The Germans always seemed to know the identity of the troops opposite them. Indeed sometimes in other sectors where the lines were only 40 or 50 yards apart they would greet us with shouts of 'Hello Kensingtons'.

I had already tried to get back to my company, but the corporal told the Transport Officer that I was one of his best pack-animal men, so my request was unsuccessful. However, my reputation as a signwriter eventually helped me to get up to the line, as I was sent for to proceed to the Pioneer Section in Hebuterne to paint the inscription on a black cross for a German airman recently shot down. Airmen were always treated with great respect and honour by both sides. Incidentally the crosses for German dead were always painted black, those for British being white.

After this I was given the task of painting the trench names on dozens of small pieces of wood for the Y and W sectors, such as Yellow Street, York Street, Wood Street, Wine Street, etc. The Regimental Sergeant Major Blake came into the barn to inspect progress and I took the opportunity to tell him I wanted to get back to company.

He said, 'Why? Is transport work too hard for you?' and I replied 'No, I like it very much, but I would prefer to be with my comrades in the trenches.'

He said, 'We will see', and next day I was attached to the Pioneer Section, comprising a sergeant, corporal and about half a dozen men, all somewhat older than myself, although I was senior in service to the privates. Three were skilled carpenters, two as bricklayers and one a plumber. We saw little of the sergeant who was usually back in the transport lines and stores, together with the sergeant tailor, shoemaker and armourer, no doubt looking after the sergeants' mess.

When in the line we were engaged on work in and about the trenches and battalion headquarters. This entailed carrying-parties for food, water and ammunition, taking barbed wire and timber to the front line, repairing revetments to the trench walls, repairing and laying duck-boards, sometimes wiring and sandbagging in no-man's land. This experience was useful to me in after life, as I learned quite a bit about carpentry, brick laying, soldering and constructing timber huts, etc.

It was a fairly free and easy existence when out of the line. We had hardly any parades or exercises and plenty of opportunity for exploring both in the trenches and in the rear areas, sometimes using our local knowledge as guides or being sent to isolated spots for about 24 hours, where we were often spotted and subjected to some close and unpleasant shell-fire. Although we could not see the object of this at the time, it must have been in order to find if such positions were under observation by the enemy.

The battalion now being so depleted in numbers, we had to take part in the stand-to in the front line for two hours every morning at dawn, a boring and unpleasant chore, particularly in pouring rain. This entailed standing still for a couple of hours, with fixed bayonets, in case of an enemy attack, which up to that period would almost invariably be made about dawn.

Now a word about Hebuterne itself. This must originally have been a very beautiful village, with its long main road, lined with pleasant cottages and a few houses, surrounded by orchards and gardens, an old church with tower, and several farm-houses. The main road ran parallel with the front line, that side being originally well wooded. At the T road junction with the road to Sailly-au-bois, (about 2 or 3 miles distant) was a small Royal Engineers unit with a large circular saw, often in use cutting tree-trunks into posts for trench revetments and duck-boards, etc. How it escaped being destroyed by shell fire I do not know. Along the right of the main road was a brick mill building, used as our advanced battalion headquarters, with cooks, signallers, runners, and so on. Leftwards the road was lined with cottages and houses.

We were billeted in a derelict farmhouse at the end of the village alongside the road. An archway led into the usual square courtyard, a huge cess-pool in the centre with a wide pathway all round and a water pump facing the entrance. The water, in common with that of all French farms, was only a few feet distant from the cess-pool, the water being quite yellow and undrinkable. The surface of the cess-pit appeared solid, but woe betide anyone who stepped on it and broke the surface, for they would sink into the liquid contents and the stench would be horrible, being composed of centuries of stable manure, cow dung and house refuse. Dead animals were often left to rot and sink into these pits, which could be smelt for miles around whenever opened up and contents extracted and spread over the fields.

The entrance side of the building was an open shed with lofts above. The other three sides were living quarters, barns, stables and cowsheds, all facing the central cess-pit. This village was of course deserted, but in the occupied farms, nearly all of this type, the farmer and family would sit at meals at a window facing on to the courtyard, oblivious to the sight and effluvia of the pit. Practically every dwelling and building in the village had been damaged by shell-fire. The church was in ruins, but the tower, which must have afforded a magnificent view over the battlefield and beyond, was more or less intact in spite of frequent shelling. It was unhealthy to linger in its vicinity owing to this, although I ventured a look around it a couple of times. Battalion HQ had a wall of sand-bags in front of it as protection from the nightly strafe from long range German machine guns, which would traverse the whole length of the road, probably half a mile long, and it was very dangerous walking along it at night, the bullets sounding like bees, Tz, Tz, Tz, with occasionally Trrr – Trrr as they ricocheted off walls or trees, and thudding into walls as one passed, keeping fingers-crossed hoping not to 'stop one'.

I had many a long walk along this road in the evening, when we took it in turns to fetch rations and post from HQ. One night as I approached HQ I heard moans coming from the ditch alongside, and found a man wounded badly by machine gun bullets. Two other chaps happened to be passing and recognised him as one of the cooks.

The surrounding fields and remains of orchards were inundated with shell holes, smashed trees and outbuildings. There were many unexploded shells lying about, some of large calibre. I saw one stupid man trying to remove the brass nose-cap from one with a chisel. We gave him and the shell a wide berth. Perhaps he was fed-up with life!

At first we slept in a large barn behind the farm. One night a whizz-bang shell hit a corner of the roof, blowing a hole through it. The funny thing was that I slept through this episode and only knew about it in the morning when I woke and asked about the hole. The other occupants were amazed that I had slept through the explosion. After this we moved into what must have been a stable in the farm courtyard. Inside this the French soldiers, who originally held the line here, had dug about 3ft. down from floor level and built a dugout neatly constructed of sand bags. One of them had left a blue French overcoat in a corner on top of the dugout. We slept on the floor of the stable and only used the rather cramped dug-out if shelling was too near and severe.

The latrine was in the orchard at the back of the farm, and every morning, when it was most in use, the Germans would fire one or two whizz-bangs into the orchard. The devils must have known what was there. Naturally our visits were made very hurriedly and brief. The enemy seemed to know almost everything about us and our movements. An observer plane was frequently overhead, and one was actually brought down in an adjacent field and we hurried over and had a look at the airman, who was uninjured.

On the other side of our courtyard the Regimental Police were ensconced in a similar room, near the entrance archway. The door and the entrance to the inner dugout was adjacent to the archway. These chaps slept in the dugout which was larger than ours.

Two field kitchens were moved into the yard, and we hoped these were not spotted by the enemy airmen and mistaken for guns, thereby inviting unwelcome attention from shells.

We were instructed one day to enter a communication trench on the other side of the road. This trench was now out of use as it was under observation in daylight. Much of it had been destroyed during the recent battle, and afforded little or no cover from the German lines. We must soon have been spotted as a heavy shell fire was put down along the trench, but we managed to get through and were glad to get into the deep cover of the front line, where the corporal reported and we were immediately sent along to another point and along a deserted and battered communication trench. This led through the remains of a small wood and out to a narrow sunken lane.

We turned left and proceeded down this lane, passing some deserted trenches crossing the lane, and coming to a point looking right over no-man's land and the German trenches. We were evidently spotted here as we came under fire from a machine gun. There appeared to be no troops holding this particular section. I do not know what instructions the corporal had received, but we turned and made our way back up the lane which led to the main road of the village. Our little jaunt must have been to find out if these routes were safe to use.

On approaching our farm archway, we could smell the acrid fumes of a shell, and as we went through the entrance a strong and sickly smell of fresh blood. There were several bodies lying outside the police dugout, the khaki uniforms dark with blood. Several stretcher bearers were still at work bringing out grisly remains from the dugout.

A shell had pierced the roof and wall of the barn, crossed the arched entrance, and through the doorway of the room containing the police dugout and through the entrance of the dugout which was only about 4ft. high. Two cooks were sitting on the top step of this, watching the police inside who were playing cards. The police sergeant, an old Kensington had just popped in for a word with them. He and four of the police were killed outright, and by some miracle four others were only slightly wounded or shell-shocked, in spite of the confined space about 8ft. square. The shell had passed the heads of the two cooks without harming them.

The five bodies were laid out on stretchers in an open sided shed where they remained uncovered until the next day, and I was appalled at the sight. Some were headless, one blown off at the shoulders, some limbs were missing, just like carcases in a butcher shop, with the white of bones showing out of the torn red flesh. It was ghastly and impossible to identify them. One of the young stretcher bearers laughingly told us that he had picked hands and fingers off the walls of the dug-out. This seemed terribly callous behaviour, but I now realise that his mind must have been shocked and unhinged at the time.

There was a beautiful large cherry tree in the garden behind the farmhouse. It was loaded with ripe cherries, and had been spared by the protection of the walls of the building. The lads soon despoiled this tree of its fruit, one fellow sawing off the thick branches. The tree was ruined in the process. The German airman had been buried near this tree.

Running along against the farm wall was a narrow trench which had been dug by the French troops. Sticking out from the trench side were the remains of a soldier, parts of the blue uniform, the decomposed remains of a knee and a hand. It was quite usual for the French to bury their dead in the trench sides, and we would sometimes uncover such grizzly remains when digging.

A rather amusing incident occurred at a house a few doors away from the farm. This was used as a sergeants' mess, and they had fitted up a table in what had been the front garden. From some mysterious source they had acquired a large white tablecloth and one afternoon a sumptuous tea had been laid for them, when suddenly a whizz-bang landed in the garden, demolishing the splendid spread. An airman had no doubt spotted the white cloth and directed the artillery. It was a remarkably fine piece of accurate ranging, but not so surprising as the Germans must have by now been familiar with every foot of the village, both from maps and air observation.

There were several trench raids carried out at night-time at this period, the object being not only to harass the enemy, but to capture one or two prisoners for identification, or to destroy machine gun posts, etc. There were also fighting patrols to meet and attack German patrols, and reconnaissance patrols to obtain information but avoid contact with the enemy. Also there were listening posts, for lying with an ear against a bayonet stuck in the ground for sounds of activity such as digging or wiring. There were wiring parties to repair or lay barbed wire entanglements.

The noisy method of hammering in angle iron stakes for holding the wire was to be superseded by screw pickets, a much more efficient and quieter method. In addition to this there was sentry duty on the fire-step, 'standing-to' for an hour or so every dawn and sunset and such chores as digging and repairing trenches, revetments, duck-boards and sumps, carrying parties for rations, ammunition, wire and so on. The troops were therefore pretty well occupied.

At first the men for bombing raids were volunteers. Before the raid all identification symbols such as regimental flashes were removed, personal belongings such as pay-books, letters, etc. had to be left behind. Faces were often blackened, noisy accoutrements left behind, weapons would be hand grenades and coshes, some carrying rifles, a light machine gun (Lewis gun) for covering fire, wire cutters, soft cap or woollen helmet, and so on. Later on, in snowy weather, white overalls would be issued.

We had a very brave Major (Campbell) who used to wander about in no-man's-land at night time, with his walking stick and batman for company. He was wounded seven times and seemed to bear a charmed life. He was very highly admired by all.

Another fine man was our C of E padre, who would go out into no-man's-land at night with the burial parties and say a few prayers over the dead. At one time we had a RC padre, who was not popular, as far as I know never leaving the safety of the transport lines and drinking copious bottles of whisky.

We were now getting large drafts of men from England, some returning from hospital. Many of the new arrivals, much to our dismay, were from other regiments, but they soon settled down as Kensingtons. We actually had a draft of 20 men from the Bantams, much to our amusement, but they also merged well with us. One draft of 200 men was entirely composed of men from other units, while an equal number of Kensingtons went to other battalions. This was not good for 'esprit de corps' and seems incompetence by higher authorities. However, later on misplaced men were able to apply for transfer to their own units.

Grisly warnings were sometimes left at the roadside as reminders of the danger of carelessness against snipers. Once a man was left on the road all day, quite uncovered, his skull being split by a snipers bullet, exposing the brains for all to see. Another time a steel helmet was mounted on a stick showing the hole made by a bullet.

Hebuterne made a haunting impression on me. As I have said before, it must have been a beautiful village before the War. It bore evidence of the French troops who had fought there before the British took over. This was a deserted ghost-like village, very eerie, but I was, and still am, endeared to it in spite of its terrible history. I would like to visit it again, but it would of course have long ago been rebuilt and lost its original charm.

At the end of August 1916 we were relieved by a Yorkshire brigade, fresh from the Somme battle-field further south, where we were now to go. They gave us much foreboding when they told us of the horrors and stress awaiting us.

After being relieved we moved to the Abbeville area for rest and training. These so-called 'rest' periods were sometimes more exhausting than when in the trenches, with long route marches, drills and so on. It was often found that after being in the trenches men were really unfit for marching and other exertions.

We here saw the tanks for the first time. These early tanks were very slow, about four miles an hour, and often breaking down. They were treated more as a joke by the infantry, causing much amusement and ridicule, although we appreciated their probable usefulness in smashing a path through the enemy wire, if they ever got so far. These wire entanglements were often very dense and wide, sometimes 40 yards or even much more. If not destroyed by artillery fire they hampered our attacks, making impenetration virtually impossible. Many a man was caught up by barbed wire and killed, left hanging on the terrible barbs. The German wire had barbs about 1 inch long, much stronger and more formidable than ours.

We soon moved to Corbie and on towards Douars, but suddenly received orders to march back to Sailly-le-Sec, quite close to the River Somme, of which we caught glimpses between the trees. The roads were crammed with French troops and transport, the country much pitted with shell-holes. The long march to Bray in the hot sun was one of the most exhausting I had so far experienced, a large number of men having to fall out on the way. We were never allowed to drink water while on the march, but were allowed the ten minute rest every hour. For the last few miles, which seemed never-ending, I felt at each step that it was impossible to go any further, but kept saying to myself 'Just one more step' at each stride and was never so grateful as when at last we reached our destination and got a welcome mug of tea and some bread, butter and jam.

We spent the night here before proceeding to the Citadel Camp the next morning. This was situated in a vast flat plain, devoid of landmarks and bare and desert-like. We sheltered in contraptions rather like chicken hutches, with rabbit wire walls. This was the site of the old British front line from which the first assault was made.

The ground was badly smashed up, and covered with horse lines and transports of other units. A huge French gun mounted on railway lines would arrive and fire a shell, immediately pulling away to some place farther back by a steam engine. I would not have cared to be a German in the vicinity of one of these gigantic shells when it burst.

That afternoon the King, riding a horse, came sight-seeing, but got no further, the front line being some seven to eight miles from the camp and much too dangerous to chance losing our monarch. His son, Edward Prince of Wales, afterwards Windsor, was soon to join us under the wing of the Grenadier Guards. I was to pass him quite closely on several occasions later on.

There were one or two intriguing sights for the King to see. One was the body of a German transfixed by a bayonet through his body to a wooden trench support. Another (which I did not go to see) was a dug-out containing the bodies of a German officer and two dead German women in nurses uniforms. I very much doubt if these were genuine relics, and am sure they were placed there deliberately for the edification of His Majesty!

While here we saw contingents of the Australian army, and a fine body of men they were. I had seen a few Australians in England at Saffron Waldon, where sometimes they would stand about in the roads practising their skill with long stock-whips.

After a night here we marched a short distance to a camp of Nissen huts at either Fricourt or Maricourt Siding, I forget which. This camp was at the edge of a plateau with a main road running past at the bottom of a cliff-like bank, and reached by a lane descending steeply at right angles to the face of the embankment. There was a great deal of movement along this road, which ran roughly parallel to the British and French front lines, about seven miles away. Parties of French infantry (poilus) would pass by, with their quick lurching step, leaning forward under heavy packs and in long sky-blue greatcoats, the bottoms of which were buttoned back at knee height. On the other side of the road were a few ruined buildings, two obviously being the remains of estaminets.

A frequent sight was a medley of horse-drawn vehicles, some being farm carts, all loaded with bandaged wounded British soldiers, coming up the inclined lane from the road and proceeding past the camp on to the field hospitals in the rear. There were so many of them that we had an uncomfortable foreboding of what was in store for us.

One of our favourite songs was:

I don't want to die, I don't want to die
I don't want to go to those trenches again,
The Allemein snipers they drive me insane,
I want to be – where those Jerries they can't snipe at me
Oh, My – I don't want to die.
I want to go home.

I think we spent a night here in the huts, the next afternoon crossing the road and entering what appeared to be a valley or large quarry, where we dumped our packs and overcoats and changed to battle order, with haversack and ground-sheet on our backs, water bottle, bayonet, entrenching tool, gas-masks, rifle, steel helmet, ammunition (60 rounds) in our pouches. We were then loaded down with other paraphernalia, such as extra cartridges in bandoliers, mills bombs, rockets and flares, some picks and shovels and so on. We were to relieve the 7th Royal Irish Fusiliers in trenches near Falfemont Farm and Leuze Wood (known to us as 'Lousy Wood').

We were now to enter an entirely different terrain to that to which we had up to now been accustomed. Before we had been used to seeing green and fertile country with green trees and woods, with villages often still occupied by at least a few civilians within a mile or so of the trenches. From here onwards for a depth of about seven miles the land was entirely bare and devastated all round, with plains and low ridges, with no greenery – most desert-like, the ground torn up and covered with shell holes, one merging in with another. The earth was greyish, with white chalk showing where the battered and flattened remains of trenches existed. The former roads and lanes no longer existed as such, rough tracks here and there, cut up and trodden by transport, gun limbers and infantry. There was a great deal of debris on the surface, the remains of barbed wire, smashed vehicles, weapons and broken timber. Woods and copses were destroyed. Villages and farms were non-existent.

Here and there were batteries of guns of all calibres, some fully exposed in the open, many without cover or camouflage of any kind. There was an almost continuous roar of artillery fire in the distance and the sharper explosions of the guns around us. Overhead could be heard the whistle and scream of passing shells, the larger shells roaring along with the rumbling sound of railway trains. Occasionally there would be a lull in the bombardments, but gunfire would always be heard even when in more distant sectors. The expenditure in ammunition must have been colossal. Dead bodies were still lying about in differing states of decomposition. These were mainly German, the British dead having been mostly buried or disposed of, although there were still many of these lying around. Dead horses were to be seen along the tracks, sometimes whole teams of them, horribly mutilated. The stench was awful. When one realises that the British alone suffered 60,000 casualties on the first day of the Somme battle, and the fighting had by now been going on for two months, the devastation was perhaps not surprising.

Ascending from the quarry we emerged onto a large flat plain which had apparently been cleared of the debris of battle. There seemed at first nothing of interest around us, except that I noticed lying on the ground a few small bones, undoubtedly finger bones, looking rather old and brown. I wondered whether these were from a casualty, or if the site had been an old cemetery now obliterated. Further on we came across the body of a young French soldier, in blue greatcoat and his rifle beside him. His body could not have been there very long and he had probably been killed by shrapnel. It was rather mystifying why he should have been there and why he had not been found and removed.

We went on past a shattered wood and on to a rough track, guns and limbers moving both up and down this thoroughfare, with occasional walking wounded and stretcher cases coming down from the line. We were led off in single file by guides from the Irish Rifles, and headed by our officers. Darkness had now fallen, and we were told to try and keep a hand on the shoulder of the man in front, so as not to lose touch. The horizon ahead was lit up for miles, as we could see whenever we passed over a ridge, and around us were the flashes and detonations of our own artillery as they fired. Figures of stretcher bearers could be seen struggling with their burdens, silhouetted against the sky – the going, over ground pitted with shell holes, wire and debris, being so arduous over the

'The Kensingtons at Laventie' from the painting on glass by Eric Kennington. Corporal J. Kealey is about to give the order 'Fall in No. 7 Platoon'. In the first four reading from right to left are Private Slade, resting with both hands on his rifle; Lance Corporal Wilson, Private Guy and Private McCafferty who is turning to look at the other men falling in behind. On the extreme left is Private H. Bristol. Directly behind Private Guy are two men in waterproof sheets, Private Kennington (the artist) in a trench helmet and Private W. Harvey. On the ground is Private A. Todd—he has fallen exhausted by continual sickness, hard work, lack of sleep, and long hours of 'standing-to' and observing.

Merville 1915. *From left to right:* Billy Hewitt (later wounded), the author (later wounded) and Arthur Budge (later killed).

miles that eight bearers were necessary for each stretcher. The suffering of the wounded must have been great, as the bearers often stumbled or fell in to the holes or old trenches. The passage of some of the shells overhead could be traced by what seemed a red spark.

This should have seemed terrifying to me, but I had not yet learned the cold, belly-gripping fear, almost paralysing the senses, that I was at times later to experience. Peculiarly enough, I was not to encounter this extreme fear until about a year later. I think this was fairly common, the longer one survived the more the fear would be felt. It is well known that often young inexperienced troops will attack with the utmost abandon and dash, the survivors becoming less enthusiastic and more cautious as experience is gained. The novelty and strange and interesting happenings helped to keep one's mind off the immediate dangers until they became more commonplace. I must confess that at that time warfare seemed rather thrilling and heroic to me. I was soon to realize that there was little or no glory in war – it was a horrible and evil thing, carried out in the midst of corruption and filth defying description, and a shocking wastage of young life. The tales of glorious battles, heroic deeds, martial music and smart parades, which I had read of and seen in my boyhood days were shortly to bring disillusionment and sadness into my life.

The route was more than seven miles, but it took us over fifteen hours to get to our destination. We could only proceed at a snail's pace in the dark, stumbling into and around shell craters, tripping over barbed wire and other debris, with frequent stops as those in the rear called for a halt to enable the stragglers to catch up. We were continually passing back messages to those behind, such as 'Mind the hole', 'Mind the wire', our voices becoming mechanical mumbles as we got weaker and sleepier. There were occasional long stops when the guides lost their way. Some of the men actually fell asleep while standing and had to be prodded awake to carry on. At one long stop I sat down for a rest in the dark. When it was time to move on I shook the shoulders of the fellow lying next to me to try and wake him, and realized he was stiff and dead. When returning past this spot some time later, I saw that he was not only dead, but only his upper half was there, his lower half having been completely blown away. He was one of the Irishmen and had been killed before our arrival.

We were now very near our destination. Dawn found us at the end of a valley. Turning left we entered another long narrow valley with steep sides to both flanks. This was named Angle Wood Valley, known to us as 'Death Valley'. The top of the ridge on our left had shallow dug-outs and strong points overlooking the huge plain over which we had travelled. On the right was a steep embankment facing the enemy lines, and half way along the ridge of the valley was a small shattered wood or copse called Wedge Wood. The far end of the valley rose to Leuze Wood, or as we called it, 'Lousy Wood'.

As we entered Death Valley there lay the bodies of two Germans, one an NCO and the other either an officer or Regimental Sergeant Major of the Prussian Guard, wearing a very fine uniform. He was a magnificent figure of a man, fair haired and in his prime. I had a feeling of sadness to see the end of such a fine specimen of manhood.

Nearby was a small steam engine. A light railway had evidently once run through this valley, but the rails were now missing, probably sent to Germany for turning into guns or shells. Behind us we could see a sunken road running up-hill and sheltering a battery of heavy guns of the French artillery. Big Jack Johnson shells would occasionally burst near them with large clouds of black smoke. These guns were about 400 yards away and we could see the French artillerymen running like rabbits to their dug-outs as soon as a shell arrived.

We were here on the extreme right of the British army and next to a French battalion. At the junction of the two valleys was an abandoned machine gun post, now only containing a pile of empty cartridge cases. Here and there were small heaps of the light blue French hand grenades about the size of small round oranges. Not understanding their mechanism we gave them a wide berth.

As we commenced the relief in the morning the remnants of the Royal Irish Fusiliers came drifting back over the ridge into Death Valley, in twos and threes. Many of them were in a very exuberant and excitable mood, claiming that they had advanced a mile over their objective, which later proved rather an exaggeration, although I believe they had indeed passed their original objective for a considerable distance. Their losses had been heavy indeed, 350 casualties, which was half their strength. Their attack had reached a cornfield in front of Combles, the corn concealing a trench protected by a formidable barbed wire entanglement, and they had been forced to retire some distance and take a position in shell holes about Falfemont Farm and in Leuze Wood. There were no dugouts or other shelter available and advanced battalion head-quarters had to make do with a shell-hole, a most inconvenient and unsuitable place for the Colonel and his staff to operate from.

My section filed to the top of the ridge and emerged on to an open slope, much cut up by shell-fire, and overlooking a wide vista of country descending to low ground, beyond which were green fields and thick wooded hills rising in the distance several miles away. This was the first green country we had seen since our leaving the Citadel, seven or eight miles behind. The ground just over the ridge of Death Valley was scattered with the Irish dead, mainly young fellows who mostly appeared to have been killed by concussion, tiny streaks of blood having issued from their ears and noses. Others had been killed by machine gun and shrapnel fire. There were hundreds of bright unexploded shells lying around, all pointing towards our position. These apparently had been fired point blank at the Irish, and due to the flat trajectory the nose caps had not struck the ground, thus failing to explode. One middle aged Irishman was sitting upright in a shell hole, one side of his head shining pink, where half his scalp had been torn off. It was a mystery how he was in a sitting position, as normally he would have collapsed on being killed. Perhaps his bayonet scabbard was propping him up. Nearby a pure white woollen toy dog was lying. This had probably been taken over by one of the attackers as a mascot.

On the left of the ridge was the remains of a small wood or copse, Wedge Wood if I remember rightly. We turned left and entered a trench running alongside. This trench was full of German dead, Prussian Guards. For some peculiar reason they were minus their tunics, wearing new white vests. The bodies were lying several deep, and we had to walk on them in order to proceed along the trench. It was apparent that they had only arrived in the line just before the attack, otherwise they would not have been in such a clean condition. It was a most unpleasant and queazy feeling having to step on these bodies, but I was to become used to this sort of thing before long, when we became hardened to such conditions and lost our feelings of revulsion. Some of the dead had their clothing burnt off them.

We reached the line of shell-holes running at right-angles to the trench and took over from the remainder of the Irishmen. The immediate task was to join up the shell holed positions by digging with our entrenching tools and forming a rough trench – now our front line. Our pioneer section, a corporal and eight men, including myself, were instructed to set off back the seven miles to the camp at Maricourt. I cannot remember now for what purpose, but think it was to fetch rations and water back to the line. We had received no food for about twenty hours and felt famished.

On reaching the ridge above Death Valley we stopped and searched some of the dead men's haversacks for food. I found a tin of sardines, army biscuits and butter. We felt rather guilty and squeamish about this, but we did get a bite of food. An officer passing in the valley below shouted to us to get down, as we would be seen by the enemy. We probably had been, but were mistaken for stretcher bearers and left unmolested. I shared the sardines with my chum, Dick Sweet, a sturdy young fellow of about my own age. We had all paired off in couples. The sitting corpse had now collapsed.

Going down to the floor of the valley we passed one or two German dead, including the aforementioned officer and another NCO with a red cord at his shoulder, which I was tempted to cut off as a souvenir, and as we passed the old steam engine a Jack Johnson shell landed about 30 yards away, exploding in a huge black cloud of smoke, but fortunately doing us no harm. We had probably been seen while on the ridge, or more probably from the German 'sausage' balloon, a good distance away, but with a clear view down the length of the valley, and up the sunken road occupied by the French artillery. At the end of the valley was a small dug-out, passing which we heard some feeble groans. Looking inside we found a badly wounded German, but he seemed far too gone for us to do anything for him. We turned right and commenced the seven mile walk back to camp – this time in daylight, coming across the trunk of the soldier I had endeavoured to wake up the previous night.

On the way back we had a good view of the old battlefield and the evidence of the furious and stubborn struggles which had so recently taken place over it. The debris of broken rifles, remnants of barbed wire, pieces of shell – some enormous and big enough to cut a man in two. The land was rolling, with low ridges, and occasional devastated woods, all that was left of them being stunted and split trunks with no foliage. There were no buildings, any house or farm no longer existent except as brick rubble and wood, shelled level with the ground.

Batteries of artillery were exposed in the open, some of them firing salvos or drumfire, the gunners working like furies at times, stripped to the waist, carrying shells, loading and firing; the men on the big howitzers turning and covering their ears each time the gunner holding the firing lanyard made a half-turn to fire his gun. If one stood immediately behind a large howitzer the shell could be seen rising like a cricket ball on its journey to the Jerries. Some batteries were concealed in camouflaged gun pits and were almost impossible to see unless close up. Crossing a track within a yard or so of one battery, which did not appear to be in action at the time, I was following a fellow about two yards in front of me when the gun fired immediately between us at about waist level. The blast was terrific and unexpected. One step forward and I would have been blown in half. I do not know whether the gunners were not aware of us or could not care less.

We arrived at the quarry, passing our dumped packs, crossed the road and ascended the path to the top of the embankment and on to the camp. Here we got a hot meal and a welcome rest until later in the afternoon we gathered our burdens and returned to Death Valley before nightfall, having traversed over twenty miles of rough ground with no sleep for thirty-six hours. We settled down on the ground at the side of the valley and slept, although there was a heavy bombardment going on in the vicinity. Several times afterward we were going to go for seventy hours or so without sleep, the feeling of carrying on while totally exhausted being pretty awful.

There now began a period of confusion and muddle, due to the shocking incompetence and worse by Brigade Headquarters, situated several miles behind the line and comfortably installed in deep dug-outs of German origin. It appears that our battalion, since taking over from the Royal Irish Fusiliers, were under temporary command of another brigade, there being no proper liaison between the two. We were instructed to send a reconnaissance patrol to find if the enemy trench behind the barbed wire in the cornfield was occupied. The patrol went forward, but reported that the wire was intact and the trench in front of Combles was indeed occupied. This information was reported back to brigade, who sent us an operation order to the effect that the air-force had reported the enemy trench to be unoccupied, which our patrol, having come under heavy fire and losing one man, contradicted.

The French, on our right, whom we found were not nearly so far advanced as we were told, contacted us and supplied us with a plan showing their position, which we sent back to Brigade Headquarters. The French made an attack that night towards Combles, which failed. We moved forward in the night to endeavour to take Combles trench, but the Germans were too strong to be driven out, although we managed to keep one company forward in Leuze Wood.

A message was received from the 169th Brigade (we were by now getting orders from three different brigades all conflicting), the latter asking why we had not occupied Combles trench as ordered, and that they had received no reports from us. Our colonel *had* sent reports, but these had evidently got to the wrong brigade and had not been passed on. Also we had not been informed when the change of brigades had taken place.

No one of any of the Brigade Headquarters had been sent forward to see what was happening, apparently staying in the safety of their deep dug-outs. Most of the junior staff-officers were very young and inexperienced. Some of the senior staff, the Brigadier, Brigade Major and Captain are known to have stayed the whole of the time, when their battalions were in the line, in deep dug-outs. This has been verified later in print as craven and callous behaviour. From these dug-outs they would plan operations by map, never going out to see the actual conditions themselves. This caused much bitterness to our own officers and men and did not tend to raise confidence or morale.

This behaviour justified the words of one of our favourite songs:

If you want to find the Colonel
I know where he is, I know where he is,
I know where he is,
If you want to find the Colonel
I know where he is
Down in the deep dug-out
I saw him, I saw him
Down in the deep dug-out I saw him
Down in the deep dug-out.

It must be stressed that such incidents were rare and isolated, as many brigadier generals and also their staffs suffered a very large proportion of killed and wounded as shown in official records. This was especially so on the Ypres sector.

One of our companies had great difficulty in getting into Leuze Wood on our left, but eventually drove the enemy out, bombing along the trench and making contact with the London Scottish.

The French once more attacked Combles but again failed. Brigade told us that the village was occupied by the French and the Germans had withdrawn. This was utter nonsense. It was never taken by frontal attack, but later, as I will tell, was outflanked on either side by British and French in unison, making the enemy withdraw.

From all this you can see how muddled the situation was from the start. I am afraid that my mind also is very muddled, these incidents and what followed for the next six weeks or so, together with the appalling conditions making it impossible to recall what really happened. Incidents become isolated and confused. We in the ranks, having no knowledge of the battlefield as a whole and without access to maps of any kind, had very little idea of our whereabouts and only meagre snippets of information or rumours of what was going on in our own sector. Often one knew nothing of what was happening beyond a few yards away. After a lapse of over sixty years, some details come back to me vividly, while others are lost, and the sequence of events probably far from accurate.

Many of the things I mention are of course very gruesome, but I want this to be a true recital of the facts, so far as I remember them, otherwise the picture would be incomplete. A few of the dates and figures I have managed to verify since the War. Also the few sketch plans I have since come across have helped in clarifying overall events and situations which were not fully understood by me at the time.

The strain of being subjected to heavy shell-fire for sustained periods, hours and sometimes days and nights almost without cessation, was enormous. One had to try and shut everything from one's mind and to become oblivious to what was going on around. There was a feeling of having a tight violin string in one's head which was due to snap at any instant and drive one insane.

The Germans of course, having occupied all this territory for a year or two before being driven back, knew the positions of all their old trenches and dug-outs as well as landmarks and could range their artillery fire with extreme accuracy. They were also able to retire to strong and carefully prepared trenches and dug-outs, also well protected and concealed gun positions.

We on the other hand were exposed in desolated territory, terribly cut up by shell-fire, all roads and houses destroyed. Also our artillery were exposed in the open for miles back and under observation from aircraft and sausage balloons. Our supplies and ammunition were extremely difficult to get up to the line, particularly in wet weather and in the night, in thick mud and water-logged shell holes. Guns and horse-drawn vehicles would get stuck or overturned in shell-holes. Motorised traffic was an impossibility on the Somme and only used on the more or less intact roads many miles in the rear. The procedure of the walking wounded was pitiful indeed as also for the stretcher cases and their bearers whose hands were often blistered and bleeding. Conditions therefore were always a hundred times worse for advancing troops than for their opponents.

One difficulty was the passing back of messages and receipt of instructions from Brigade. We had no wireless at this period and the signallers were kept busy continuously in repairing and laying telephone wires along or in the ground, these being cut by shell-fire almost as soon as they were laid. The signallers' job was not to be envied, with constant hard work often in very dangerous conditions. A very exasperating and discouraging job. Messages had therefore to be carried also by runners, who often had to go through several heavy barrages both during the day and at night. Each company and also Battalion headquarters had its own runners. Pigeons were sometimes used by Brigade and Divisional headquarters, but not very successfully. Messages did not always get through for obvious reasons.

The old German dug-outs had been very well constructed, but most had been destroyed or blocked at the entrances or steps, and sometimes befouled with dead. Also the entrances faced the wrong way for us, being vulnerable to shell-fire. There was always the nasty prospect of being buried alive in them. A few of the largest and deepest had two entrances to them. The Germans would usually shelter the bulk of their troops in these dugouts during heavy shelling, coming to the surface at the last minute or two to oppose our attacks. Sheltering in a dug-out had a very demoralising effect, as feeling comparatively safe while underground, it gave one a horrible and terrifying feeling to emerge into the danger, and it needed all one's willpower to do so. Many a time the enemy refused to come up to the trench to surrender or fight, in which case grenades would be pitched down the entrances to kill the inmates. It was too dangerous to leave armed enemy in the rear. The support troops following closely on the first lines would complete this task, called 'mopping up'.

On losing their first line, the enemy would put down a heavy barrage on this, and also on the supporting troops, endeavouring to prevent them from reaching the assault troops with reinforcements and much needed bombs and ammunition, and to try and prevent the second wave of attackers from leap-frogging our first objective and assaulting the enemy support lines. Very heavy casualties were usually suffered by the supporting troops, as we had found to our cost at Hebuterne. Counter attacks were then expected, launched from the comparatively fresh German reserves waiting under cover of their deep dug-outs to emerge and attack our weakened and depleted force.

This was more or less normal procedure for organised attacks, but there were very many small isolated engagements, often of intense ferocity to take or regain parts of trenches or outposts which intruded into or threatened the continuity of a line. Often contact became broken between different units, or even between companies of the same battalion, one party having no idea of the position or distance separating it from the next, leaving gaps in the defence and the dangers of enfilade fire or attack. Efforts would have to be made to establish contact, and led to close combat with hand grenades to drive the enemy out along trenches or from shell-hole positions.

Unfortunately it was seldom that a major attack proceeded as successfully as originally planned. On many sectors the attacking force would be held up or even driven further back by enemy counter attacks, resulting in much confusion and loss of contact. There being no such thing as wireless communication in those days, contact had to be attempted by reconnaissance patrols.

An instance of this occurred during one advance planned to straighten out the line between Leuze Wood and Ginchy. Our 'B' Company lost touch with an Irish battalion on our left, which was afterwards found not to have reached anywhere near the position it was intended to take, having been held up by a very strong German position known as the Quadrilateral. Major Dickens (a grandson of Charles Dickens) endeavoured to lead a party further to the left to contact the Irish, but was unsuccessful and was killed in the attempt. A year later I was to revisit this place and help to erect a wooden cross and rail, which I had painted with an inscription in Old English.

Before an attack is launched on a heavily defended position it is most essential that the wide band of barbed wire entanglements is breached, very heavy bombardments being necessary for this, often over several days' duration. Also that the trench is destroyed as much as possible and machine gun emplacements obliterated, long range guns being employed in trying to locate and knock out enemy batteries in the rear, over a depth of several miles. Unless wire is properly destroyed or lanes cut through it is almost impossible for the attack to succeed, and very heavy losses will be sustained, all to no purpose. Patrols are sent out at night to try and cut through the wire, a highly dangerous operation. The attacking force held up by wire can be mown down by machine gun fire and grenades thrown or fired from the trench. Very often it was found that the entanglements had not been properly destroyed.

Since 1st July the battle had raged back and forth, each side contesting every yard of the terrain, many places being fought on over and over again, until the British and French gradually forced back the opposing forces. So dreaded was the Somme battle that it was described by the Germans in letters home as 'the bath of blood'.

We buried our dead in the vicinity of the trenches. It was difficult enough to get our wounded back to the rear areas, and impracticable if not impossible to do so with the deceased. The German dead were left where they fell, and only removed to a nearby shell-hole if or when their presence became too obnoxious. We had neither the time nor energy to expend on them otherwise. I remember four of us being detailed to bury a young fellow lying at the edge of Leuze Wood. We dug a shallow grave for him. My companions were loath to put the first spadeful of earth over him and we had nothing with which to cover his face. The job had to be done, and I placed the first few spadefuls of earth in, keeping my eyes averted, and thus buried my first man. A few minutes later we had completely forgotten the incident, there being other and more pressing events to occupy our attention. I found that however bad or terrifying anything was, it was rapidly forgotten – there was so much else to divert our thoughts.

One grisly experience was that of a young man who crawled back into the trench the day after taking part in an attack. He had been concussed by a shell and came to with his face sticking to something and naturally assumed that he had been wounded in the head. He found however, that he had fallen on to a dead German whose scalp had been blown off, his cheek sticking to the dead man's head by congealed blood. The shell burst had otherwise not injured the fellow, who appeared to have taken the shock very well except for somewhat excited repetitions of his story.

We never knew what day it was – except when out of the line church parade was ordered. I am afraid I dodged most of these, declaring that I was an agnostic, in spite of the CE stamped on my identity disc, which sometimes the orderly corporal insisted on verifying.

I must tell here of the curious episode of the Indian Cavalry. When we first entered the Leuze Wood end of Angle Wood (or Death) Valley, it was littered with cavalry swords and dozens of round folding helmets. I thought at first that these were German Uhlan helmets, but these on examination were found to belong to Indian Cavalry, the names of the now defunct owners being written on the insides. Many of the swords, and also some rifles were sticking upright in the ground, evidently marking graves. There were no bodies or horses lying about. These latter probably had been dragged away by the Germans for their fat and hides, which were in a very short supply in Germany. The relics were scattered on the floor and sides of the narrow valley.

The right hand embankment rose steeply to Leuze Wood, while at this end the opposite bank was shallow leading to a plain towards the Ginchy and Les Boeufs sectors. Scattered over the floor of the valley at this place were a large number of four pronged iron spikes about 4 inches long. I have never before or after seen these objects, which we assumed had been intended to cripple the horses, and the enemy had obviously been well aware in advance of the likelihood of a cavalry attack. The whole of this episode was a mystery to me, and I have never been able to find out the true story of the occurrence. I was tempted to keep one of the small folding helmets as a souvenir, but every one I examined had been befouled. The Indians had evidently been trapped here and mown down by the machine gun fire from Leuze Wood. Cavalry were on the whole completely useless in this war owing not only to the shell torn ground and wire entanglements, but also their extreme vulnerability to shell and machine gun fire.

I had by this time become practically immune to the sight of death and terrible wounds. It would have been impossible to keep sane otherwise.

A shell one day fell into a trench nearby, partly blowing off a man's arm above the elbow. Someone fixed a tourniquet with a putty and with his jack-knife cut off the arm completely, as it would evidently have to be done eventually. I am sure I would have jibbed at doing this.

Besides the mud and discomfort, the horrible stench of

corruption, high explosive and chloride was always in our nostrils. Our clothing was permeated with the smell, which would remain evident for a week or so after leaving the battle area. I was very surprised to see the change of colour in the corpses at various stages of decomposition. This would be either white, yellow, green, blue, red, brown and even black. Some were skeletons with a parchment like covering of skin. Maggots and blue-bottles filled the eye sockets, nostrils and mouths. The sight of blue-bottles alighting on us or our food was nauseating. Our RSM would sometimes have a biscuit tin of chloride of lime and would himself scatter this in adjacent shell-holes and pollution. We all suffered badly from dysentery due to the dirty water and contaminated food.

We were relieved from time to time, going back to reserve trenches for a few hours or a day or so, but were still under shell-fire. These places were named Maltzhorn Farm, Casement Trenches, Chimpanzee Trench, and Waterlot Farm. I am confused today as to which was which, but got a very good idea of the lie of the land and a sense of direction for some miles around, which was useful later on, especially at night time, when a couple of us would sometimes be sent as runners with messages to Brigade headquarters or to collect something at a dump, such as rations, ammunition or water in petrol tins. Water was very scarce, tainted with petrol and chlorinated. The chloride of lime was often over strong, often being added twice – once at Brigade and again by our own medical orderly, and almost undrinkable. There was never enough to wash with and we were always filthy. Sometimes we would try to wash with water from puddles or shell-holes, once or twice risking tea-making from shell-hole water, which of course was always contaminated. It is a good job that our inoculations were so efficient.

We were never allowed to remove our boots and after 2 or 3 weeks our feet were in an awful state. I did chance taking my boots off once, but my socks were stuck hard to my feet, which were bleeding and so swollen that it was with great difficulty that I managed to get my boots on again, in spite of their large size. Many men suffered so badly from 'Trench feet' when the weather and mud became really bad, that they had to become casualties. One had to be in an absolutely hopeless condition for this. Most of us were half crippled when we finally left the Somme and could only hobble along.

I remember the day when the pioneer section were sent to an isolated position on a high ridge beside a track alongside the remains of a farm, only part of a long brick wall still standing. About 50 yards from this wall was a short trench at right angles to the top of the ridge, the trench being full of German dead, with some lying on top of the parapet. We settled down in a small piece of trench, but soon moved a few yards away, as there was a dead horse on the track nearby, making an appalling stench. We could see over an extensive area on the British side, which seemed deserted, with no movement or sign of life. We did not attempt to look over the other side of the ridge. After a while we were subjected to some uncomfortably close shelling, evidently having been spotted. I had reason to be glad of my steel helmet, as a piece of high explosive shell hit it with a 'clonk'. I picked up a piece of shell, dropping it immediately as it was still hot. In the evening a runner arrived to tell us to get back.

This seemingly useless task must have been to discover whether the position was under observation by the enemy. We were in fact used as sitting ducks.

We were moved to different parts of the line between Leuze Wood, Ginchy and Les Boeufs and took part in numerous operations. I am and indeed was at the time very confused about the whole thing – quite understandable when even our own battalion officers often did not know exactly where we were, what we were supposed to be doing, and what was happening on each side of us. There were often large gaps between units. We had a draft of 50 men and two officers fresh from England and quite inexperienced. Their guides either lost their way or disappeared and the whole draft walked straight into the German lines – we never even saw them or heard of them again.

The battalion's complement of tools had now been mostly lost or destroyed, and Dick Sweet and I were sent back some miles to an Australian camp to replenish these. We arrived at what looked like a one street wooden shanty town, reminiscent of a wild west cowboy town, with various stores, a blacksmith shop and so on. This place was full of Australian personnel, wagons and horses.

One of our limbers was waiting, and we loaded this with about 40 spades, picks and axes. Before it drove off a German plane flew close overhead and dropped a small bomb a little further off up the road. I don't know if it caused any damage. Before trudging back we found an Australian canteen built in a small copse. Hoping to buy something to supplement our meagre rations we were disappointed when the surly canteen sergeant refused us, as we were not Australians. The only thing he let us buy was a pack of playing cards.

In the first week we lost over 300 men, including 15 officers, and another 50 men when out in reserve trenches. One whole platoon was destroyed by one huge shell, a Jack Johnson.

Further frontal attacks were attempted by our division and the French on Combles, but again without success. It was then decided to attack it on each flank. The London Scottish and the Fusiliers led the attack around Bouleaux Woods, the French attacking the other side of Combles. The Quadrilateral strong point had by now been captured by the Guards, thus protecting our left flank from enfilading fire which had held up previous assaults. Four tanks were to take part, but three of them broke down at the start and the fourth was soon hit by a shell. The Kensingtons were in support. This time everything went well. The British and French broke through on each side, forcing the Germans to withdraw from the village, the London Scottish joining up with the French in Combles.

I shall always remember a London Scot being carried back on a stretcher, a blanket over his lower half saturated in blood, but singing lustily:

If you're going back to Blighty,
If you're going back to Town,
In Trafalgar Square, greet the lions there
Shout 'Hallo, 'Hallo London,
Give the man in blue a fiver
Kiss the girls, don't be afraid
Tell every Western Pet
That she's not forgotten yet
By the boys of the Old Brigade.

I do not know where he got the strength to sing so lustily – it may have been from a tot of rum which can at times work wonders.

Another thing which I will never forget is a party of Queen's Westminsters coming down through Wedge Wood. Conditions had been very wet and the mud awful. They filed painfully and slowly down the slope, between the shattered tree stumps, like so many living corpses, their faces white, with eyes fixed and staring as if they had just seen into the depths of hell. God knows what they had been through.

A large area was prepared to hold German prisoners a couple of miles or so behind our lines. This was cordoned off by a high barbed wire fence. After the capture of Combles this was filled with hundreds of prisoners. Most of these seemed quite resigned and obviously glad to be out of the turmoil, but there were a few, mainly dark haired Bavarian types, sitting sorrowfully with heads in hands – surly and morose. The bulk of the prisoners appeared to be mild, harmless looking persons, who would be better spending their time in their civilian occupations, and seemed out of place in the sloppy ill-fitting grey uniforms of the German army. The German field service uniform always seemed to me to be most depressing and convict like. The British and French uniforms were much smarter, even in the worst conditions, and much more inducive to good morale.

One day when I was with the pioneer section in Death Valley, a runner came from the Regimental Sergeant Major asking for two men to report to him in Leuze Wood. I and another fellow nick-named Tubby were detailed to go, and we set off with the runner. Much to his objection we chose to go along the top of the ridge (a very foolish procedure), and the runner left us to make our own way, he choosing the safer route along the bottom of the valley. From the ridge we could see over the descending ground to the distant forest beyond the German lines on our right. An officer spotting for the artillery was lying in a shell-hole about 50 yards away observing the shell bursts on the enemy positions. He waved frantically for us to go back down the valley, but we continued on our way.

Near the end of the valley, just below Leuze Wood was a battery of French 75's, their light quick-firing guns. These guns had only just been installed and the Frenchmen were erecting tall poles, probably for ranging purposes. They stopped work as we passed, looking at us in amazement. They probably thought we were mad to be on top of the ridge. As usual with the French 75's, half their shells seemed to be faulty, as they were exploding in the air almost immediately on leaving the guns, being more dangerous to our own troops than to the Germans.

As we approached the corner of Leuze Wood a heavy fusillade of shells burst on the wood at the point we were about to enter. I suppose it would have been wiser for us to have waited a little, but we chanced it and scampered forward to the low parapet and into a clearing some 50 yards square, which had been dug about 6 feet below the surrounding ground inside the corner of the remains of Leuze Wood.

The shells were falling fast and furious and much too close to be healthy. We dived towards the entrance of the first of two dug-outs on our left. Tubby hesitated at the entrance, so I darted down the first few steps when a shell burst right outside the entrance, and I heard my companion slithering down the steps behind me.

I thought he must have been hit, so turned and called out, 'Are you all right, Tubby?' and was relieved to hear his reply in the affirmative.

We got down to the bottom of about twenty steps and entered the large dug-out. The RSM and a few runners and signallers were seated around a table in candlelight. They said that Jerry must have seen us coming (which was not surprising) hence the shelling which went on for quite a long time. The RSM handed us each a mug with about $\frac{1}{3}$rd pint of neat rum, really firewater. Two shells landed immediately on top of the dug-out, each time blowing out the candles and seeming like a sledge hammer driving our heads down about six inches. The roof was about 15 feet thick and luckily stood up to the high explosive. We spent the time chatting and our mugs were replenished with rum several times, the RSM of course being in charge of the rum ration. It is a marvel we were able to keep sober. The next dug-out was occupied by the Colonel and his staff. The two dug-outs were no doubt connected.

After the bombardment had subsided the RSM told the two of us to come outside with him, and we stood at the entrance for a few minutes while he gazed around. The rum had a marvellous effect on me and I remember saying, 'Where are those ruddy Germans, let's get at them.' I was really wanting to attack the whole German army single handed, and had to be restrained by the sergeant major, who handed me his sandbag, of 'moshings' to look after. There was a bundle of candles in the top (as precious as gold) and I slipped a couple of handfuls into my pockets when his back was turned. I would not have dared to do this if I had been sober, for we feared the wrath of the RSM more than anything. I know now that given a large tot of rum and the opportunity, how easy it would be to earn a VC or DCM. A very different matter however without the rum. The RSM asked where was our sergeant!

Incidentally just here at the corner of the wood stood, amongst other stumps, a tall tree-trunk with a wooden look-out seat high up. It must have given a wonderful view of the territory for miles over the ground on which the British had advanced. Even from ground level we could see the vast devastated plain beyond Angle Wood Valley, towards Guillemont, Ginchy and Les Boeufs. The place had most likely been used as an artillery position by the Germans before the British got too close.

Over the plain we could see parties of infantry approaching in wide spaced artillery formation, evidently our relief. Their advance must have been observed from the air, but they had no interference from shell-fire and everything was pretty quiet by now. The Germans were no doubt waiting for nightfall when the relief was likely to be in operation and our trenches packed with ingoing and outgoing troops.

We descended into Death Valley, turned left and half way along found that two of our cooks had managed to get there with a field cooker. The RSM demanded a mug of tea for us, and finding that none was on tap he soundly rated the poor cooks and then proceeded to the pioneer section, who had managed to rig up a rough shelter for themselves from bits of timber and corrugated iron. We were then all led to the end of Death Valley, turning right and onto what was once the road to Guillemont. On the way we passed a large elephant iron shelter erected by the Artillery as a store. This proved later as a useful landmark in an almost featureless landscape, the road being almost unrecognisable except when here and there marked by the short stumps of what were once trees. We came at last to our destination, a group of makeshift shelters of old wood and corrugated iron. This was called Waterlot Farm, the buildings now being non existent.

After a short rest the RSM picked three of the pioneers to accompany us back to Leuze Wood.

It was now fairly late afternoon, and this time we proceeded in a direct line to the Wood, along what appeared to have been some sort of road or track just below the summit of a long ridge, which must have overlooked the Quadrilateral and Bouleaux Wood. There was much evidence of fierce fighting having taken place along this ridge. There were numerous bodies of dead Germans lying about, some half buried or drowned in shell holes, hands, heads and feet sticking out of the churned up ground. Many of the shell holes were half full of scummy and filthy water, some reddish brown with blood. One man lying on the track had evidently had his head smashed by passing wagon or gun carriage wheels, although there was no sort of traffic along here now. It would have been too dangerous in daylight and very improbable at night, being too near and exposed to the line. There were few British dead, these apparently having been buried or removed.

On arrival at headquarters' dug-outs in Leuze Wood we were told that we were to be relieved that night by, I believe, a Yorkshire Regiment, which we had seen moving up over the plain that day. The four chaps with me were detailed as guides, one to each of the four companies, and I was to wait and guide Battalion headquarter staff out of Leuze Wood and back to the reserve position at Waterlot Farm. We waited at the top of the dug-outs.

At dusk the relief started arriving and soon our companies commenced straggling into the pit, telling us that there was terrific congestion in the narrow trenches, making it very difficult for the two units to pass each other and causing a lot of blockages. To make matters worse the enemy guessed the relief had started and began heavy shelling on the trenches and communications. One young fellow lost his reason and came rushing along the top of the trench yelling in a terrified voice, 'Sergeant's dead – they've killed Sergeant.' We tried to calm him down, but he seemed completely crazy and went rushing over the parapet and away to the rear on his own. Where he eventually got to in the dark I do not know.

As the hours went by the four companies in turn were led away by the guides, going along the straight route on the ridge, which was quiet enough and not under fire. I waited alone for what seemed an interminable time at the top of the headquarters dug-out, the relieving officers having gone below to obtain the necessary information from our colonel and the adjutant, and no doubt a tot or two of whisky. Incidentally the effects of my morning dosage of rum had long worn off. The heavy shelling on the trenches had now decreased.

At last the Colonel, Major and Adjutant emerged accompanied by the runners, signallers and batmen, about twenty or so in all, and I led them over the parapet at the corner of the wood. To my discomfort I could now see that a terrific barrage of shell fire was being laid down all along the top of the ridge and I stood for a while deciding what I had better do. I felt the heavy responsibility on my shoulders of getting this precious party back in safety. Although we had not been told which route to take, I assumed that we were meant to proceed the shortest way which was straight along the ridge, as the RSM had brought the guides. I myself certainly did not relish going through such hellish shellfire, the whole ridge now an inferno, lit up with continuous flashes from the explosions. It seemed impossible that we could traverse along that terrible line of fire without getting wiped out.

I therefore decided to cut diagonally across the plain to the left and hope to recognise the Guillemont road which we had traversed in the morning. That route had been two sides of a triangle and was rather a long way. By cutting across the plain the angle would be narrowed and the journey considerably shortened. While I was considering this, one of the officers who was in a bad state of panic asked did I know the way, and several of the men were afraid I would lose them. I did not tell them the alternatives, and they certainly had no idea of the original intention of using the ridge track. Perhaps if I had told them they might have been more docile. I started off down the slope towards the other side of the valley where the bank was much lower and almost level with the plain at this point.

As soon as I moved off the windy officer started wailing that I was leading them into the German lines, when actually we were going away from them. I was astounded that these officers of rank, and also the signallers and runners were so ignorant of the terrain, as they had maps at their disposal.

Someone asked 'How do you know the way?'

To pacify them I lied, 'By the stars.'

'But the stars have moved,' said another.

The colonel who was quite cool and quiet turned to the windy officer and said sharply, 'Be quiet – he knows what he is doing.' Perhaps he knew that I did.

After a few hundred yards we came to a battery of field guns. The artillery officer was standing with a group of gunners, awaiting our approach. They were all wearing gas masks and the officer, who appeared to be very scared, said, 'Gas, Gas, put your gas masks on.' There was no smell of gas or even explosives, and our colonel told the officer sharply to take his gas mask off. He and his gunners did this, his men looking very foolish and deflated. I fancy some of them were grinning, but it was difficult to see in the dark. I feel sure this officer had mistaken us for Germans and was preparing to surrender. If the artillery had many officers of this calibre I do not wonder that the infantry were so often shelled by our own guns.

Keeping straight on across the plain, with my fingers crossed, and hearing occasional wails that I had lost my way, I was much relieved when we at last struck the road, almost indistinguishable in the dark, and turning right were now in a straight line to Waterlot Farm. We soon reached the aforementioned elephant iron hut, which proved to me that we were on the right course. There was a light in the shelter and a few men sitting inside. One of the runners insisted on going over to confirm our direction, much to my annoyance. I would like to say that I have nothing but praise for the dangerous and brave work done by our runners in the line, but was amazed at their ignorance of the terrain behind the lines on the Somme, and wondered if this was one of the reasons for messages to Brigade sometimes going astray.

It was nearly dawn when we arrived at Waterlot Farm. A number of officers and NCO's were standing to greet our arrival, which owing to the long time taken before the party had finished their conference with the relieving officers and the rather long route back, had no doubt caused some concern. I found the pioneers in a small shack and was pleased to learn that the companies had got back safely, having left Leuze Wood long before the barrage had fallen on the ridge.

Soon after, a runner came along and told me to report to the sergeant major with my mess tin. I found him sitting on the ground outside his shack. He poured me a very large portion of rum, saying, 'If you want any more come back, but don't make a fool of yourself,' which I undoubtedly would have done if I had drunk such a quantity, which afterwards I shared with the other chaps.

I did not give him an account of what had occurred, and wondered what his reaction would have been if I had told him of the route taken. Anyway he must have learned of this from the colonel or the runners. He told me to stay with the pioneer section, who were often entrusted by him to carry out special or unusual tasks. He probably felt he could rely on us, all now being fairly old hands with a good deal of experience and confidence, and no doubt tougher and steadier than many of the newly drafted men.

Next morning we moved back to Maricourt Siding and retrieved our packs and overcoats. We felt half starved, having lived mostly off hard biscuits and cheese, with an occasional tin of bully beef or baked beans between several of us, and nothing to drink but small rations of water tasting strongly of petrol and chloride. We were now handed out a chunk of pork each (the only time we had this issued). Mine was a great hunk of rancid fat with no meat to it. This was most horrible and nauseating, but I gobbled it up, feeling terribly sick in the stomach for the rest of the day.

We went along to the field cookers for a welcome pint of tea. The sergeant cook was a hulking, black looking man with an ever scowling expression. He was bullying one of the chaps about something, and feeling angry I said, 'Leave him alone, he's just come back from the line.'

The sergeant said, 'I'll put you on a charge if you're not careful,' and I replied, 'I don't care if you do – why don't you go back to company or are you too scared?'

He was staring past my shoulder, his face red and scared. I turned and found the RSM standing behind me, looking at the cook with a sardonic grin, but saying nothing. The RSM seemed to have thoroughly enjoyed the episode and the sergeant cook must have been frightened stiff of losing his cushy job. I discreetly faded out of the scene.

The battalion reformed and marched off past the Citadel camp and on to the village of Morlancourt. On the way we halted in a field opposite another battalion who were going in the reverse direction towards the line. About fifty yards away I saw a young fellow I knew from schooldays, and by some strange coincidence he recognised me at the same time. He was a good looking curly headed boy named Gilbert, my last recollection of him being of a fight he forced upon me for no reason, except that he fancied himself at fisticuffs. We were then about fourteen years old. We crossed over and met between the two columns, shook hands and went back to our respective ranks.

I had met another old school friend a week or so before. He was with a small group of artillery preparing a gun position just below Leuze Wood, probably the same battery before mentioned. I went over to greet him and cadge a cigarette. He pressed a whole packet on to me. I shall always feel grateful for this. I met him soon after the War in the lift at Leicester Square station. He had no recollection of the incident, my friend Alec Lindsey's attention being riveted on a young woman passenger in the lift.

At Morlancourt we were installed in nice dry barns – a heavenly feeling after three or four weeks in the open, exposed to all weathers. I believe we were able to get a hot bath in tubs – were issued with new shirts, vests and socks, new tunics and trousers. This seemed a good omen and we felt sure of going back to civilisation and rest in a quiet area. Most of that day was spent in sewing our shoulder flashes, the red diamond and stripes, etc. on to our new tunics. We had a good hot meal or two, when to our dismay an order arrived for us to march back to the Citadel Camp once more, for a further spell on the Somme. We returned, feeling very depressed and disappointed.

A draft of 6 officers and 200 men arrived straight from England, all having had a very short period of training, about three months, and not really hardened enough to withstand the rigours in store for them.

We had only about six officers altogether to command the

four companies, instead of the original two dozen, and most of these were young and inexperienced. Seldom during the Somme battle did we have more than six. Our finest officers were all promoted to other units, confiscated by Brigade, killed or wounded. The colonel, who had only been with us for about two months, was I believe, from a Yorkshire battalion. He seemed a nice, quiet middle aged man, but perhaps not ruthless enough for harsh warfare. I think he had the welfare of the men very much in mind, and heard that in the last few days of the battle he remonstrated very strongly against sending the utterly exhausted and half crippled battalion into a further attack over muddy torn-up ground and without the slightest possibility of success. He was soon taken away from us and to our great satisfaction we got back one of our most popular officers, Captain Shaw – now to become Lieutenant-Colonel Shaw. He was killed by a sniper on 23rd August 1918, when going forward with his runner and signaller to reconnoitre in front of our advancing lines. A very fine and gallant officer and gentleman. I remember the date, as it was the day after I obtained my discharge from the Army.

We spent a couple of days under canvas at the Citadel camp and were then sent forward to relieve the Queen's Westminsters in the old German 3rd line. The progress over the old battlefield was very difficult and arduous. Heavy rain had made a quagmire of the ground with thick mud and water filling the shell-holes, which were so numerous that they merged into each other. Orders were again suddenly changed and we were sent back to Citadel Camp – on reaching which we were at once told to move forward again to the front. The ground was so bad that it took us from 10 o'clock in the evening until 3 o'clock the following afternoon, about seventeen hours without respite of any sort. The weather worsened and the mud and water were atrocious. This time we had greatcoats with us, but these were almost worse than useless as we were absolutely sodden with rain, and the wet coats became intolerably heavy.

A planned attack had to be postponed for 48 hours, but we sent 2 companies forward to dig an assembly trench for the assault. This was a muddle from the start, the guides losing their way and disappearing in the night. The officers tried all night to locate the position, but had to return with the task unaccomplished.

Sleeping on the ground in these conditions was extremely uncomfortable to say the least. We were already absolutely soaked, and our groundsheets were useless. If we laid on them they became basins of water, and served little or no purpose on top of us as we were already saturated. Also it was extremely cold. Two men of the new draft were found dead of exposure in the morning, not having been hardened to this kind of existence.

Next night we relieved the London Scottish in the front line. I now have no idea where we were, except that the attack was to be made towards Le Transloy and its sugar refinery. Two companies were again sent forward to dig the assault trenches, but again without luck. The positions given could not be found in the dark, and probably did not actually exist except as marks on a map in Brigade headquarters dug-out, made by someone with a fertile imagination. The colonel went off to assist in the search and one company commander went forward to reconnoitre, but did not return, having been wounded. No one had the faintest idea of what was required, so the trench was not dug.

Next night however, a new assembly line was dug and the following afternoon the attack commenced in conjunction with the French troops on our right. The shocking state of the ground made movement very difficult and things went badly, although some advance was made. The Rangers and Fusiliers met devastating machine gun fire and their leading companies were almost annihilated. The Germans made fierce counter attacks and by nightfall our brigade were all back in their original positions. The French on our right had also failed. The following day the attack was resumed, but by evening we were again driven back. The operation had failed owing mainly to the weather and the poor artillery support due to the uncertainty of our positions.

This was our last effort on the Somme and we were relieved by the Royal Warwicks and Royal Irish Rifles on 9th October 1916. The battalion staggered back to the rear areas and we were taken by French motor buses to Vaux-en-Amiens.

'The efforts of all concerned had been prodigious.' The terrain and tracks were in a terrible state – guns and limbers being bogged down to their axles in mud, many having to be abandoned in shell-holes. Men and horses sweated and struggled to get guns, ammunition and rations to the troops in the line. The transport were no sooner back to their quarters than they had to start all over again. It was now that I learned of the death of my old packhorse, it being wounded in the rump and having to be shot by the corporal. One of the transport brakemen could not stand the strain, and crushed his foot under a wagon wheel in order to get back to England.

In this last period the battalion had lost four more officers and 180 men in six days, all with nothing to show for it.

Sir Douglas Haig expressed great disappointment over this last battle, saying that if successful it would have yielded much greater results than anything we had as yet attained.

As far as I know he had never been up to the battle area and seen for himself the insurmountable difficulties and terrible conditions of his troops. The 8th Division attacked over the same ground at the end of October, but with only slight gains and at heavy loss.

We spent a few days at Vaux, re-organising the battalion and sorting out the belongings of the casualties, either for redistribution or sending back of personal effects to relatives in England.

When the roll was called I discovered that of the 25 or so in our platoon at the commencement of the battle, only the sergeant and myself were left of the original platoon. I was very lucky in having spent some of the time with the pioneer section, which although having been under much heavy shell-fire at times, had escaped some of the assaults.

IV

A Quiet Front

Our next destination was to be the deserted villages of Wanel and Sorel, about twenty miles march distant. We here made ourselves comfortable in empty cottages and barns. I was billeted in an old cottage, bedding down on the brick hearth of the old fireplace. During the night I had an uncomfortable crawly feeling and got out of my blanket, lit a piece of candle and removed my shirt, out of which fell dozens of large black beetles, which soon scuttled away. I laid down again and went to sleep, and as far as I know these unwelcome guests did not return.

We did, however, meet our friends the rats once again. While on the Somme I did not see a rat or indeed any living animal, or even birds. There were of course the ever present lice and also maggots and blue-bottles. The shell-fire was evidently too much for rats and birds to endure. A year later however, when returning to the Somme battlefield we found rats had returned and made entry into all the graves of the hastily buried dead.

We then moved to Longpré and entrained for Merville, behind the Laventie front, where the battalion had received its first experience of warfare, and where I had spent such a pleasant sojourn the previous year. We used to get much fun on these rail journeys, slow as they were. At each country station the train would stop and we would sometimes beg hot water from the engine driver to pour on our mixed tea and sugar ration.

When the train was due to start the porter (or station master-cum-porter) would emerge on the platform with a small flag and trumpet, and with much frantic waving of arms and flag and blowing of horn, engage in what seemed a vicious shouting match with the engine driver. We always expected this to result in a punch-up and would lean out of the windows or doors with cheers and jeers, egging them on until the driver eventually started off. This was, however, quite a harmless and normal procedure.

Sometimes we would pass a party of Chinese labourers repairing railway lines. They looked and behaved like monkeys, laughing and fooling, pretending to attack each other with spades. These Chinese were passionately fond of bully-beef and would offer a five franc note for a tin. Five francs was a lot of money to us, and many an iron-ration changed hands, although it was a punishable offence to get caught using our iron ration without orders, which would only be given in extreme circumstances. This ration consisted of a tin of bully, a cube of Oxo, a couple of hard biscuits (similar to dogs biscuits) and a small bag of tea and sugar mixed. We often noticed the sugar bowl in a peasant's cottage containing this mixture and also Oxo cubes, and guessed there must have been quite a black market run by some of the ASC men.

After detraining at Merville, we marched a few miles to Estaires, which with La Gorgue lay about a couple of miles behind the line at Laventie. There were still civilians in Estaires and a few estaminets open. The best estaminet was always reserved for the officers, and strictly out of bounds to other ranks. I only know of one officer who would enter one of our estaminets and have a drink with the men.

My company was billeted in what had been a small theatre or cinema, provided with straw palliasses – an uncommon luxury.

It was round about this time, the end of October or early November, that I went on my first leave home after about fifteen months. I think it was for ten or twelve days. I do not remember very much of it, being rather mixed with events from the second leave, thirteen months later. About a half dozen of us entrained from Merville to Boulogne, where we spent the night under canvas with hundreds of leave-goers from other units.

Several of us were picked haphazardly as cooks, so had no opportunity to go into town. Our duty was to cook hams and brew tea for the morrows' breakfast. None of us knew anything about cooking. In the cookhouse were a number of large coppers, similar to the old fashioned kitchen copper as was then usual in our homes. We filled one with water, lit the fire, and put in several hams. We then left for a stroll around the camp and to sleep in our tents, leaving the hams to boil all night. In the morning we made dixies of tea and inspected the results of our cooking. We were dismayed to find only ham bones and masses of what looked like wet string floating about in the copper, and we fished out the bedraggled remains of the ham and served each man, about 30 or so, with a portion. A second party arrived and were served with most of the remainder, when to our consternation a third party arrived and there was practically nothing left for them. There was a good deal of annoyance and bad language over this, and it transpired that many of the first party cunningly joined the second group and obtained second helpings. We had none left for ourselves, and felt lucky to get away without assault and battery.

We were then marched off to a large warehouse to get a good hot tub and complete change of underclothing and socks, sent to the docks and embarked for home. I arrived at Harringay in the evening, a dark night, and as I walked down Chesterfield Gardens met my mother who was going to the shops. In those days the shops were open till late at night. We got home and I immediately stripped off all my uniform and underclothes onto the scullery floor, in case I had brought home any live stock and changed into my old civvies, the suit now being a tight fit. My father and sister arrived home and we had plenty to talk about, but I am afraid I was not very articulate in those days and must have given a very garbled account of my experiences.

You can imagine how wonderful it was to be back with my beloved family again. I went up to Piccadilly next day with my mother, visited the Paymaster and drew out the £8 due to me together with subsistence allowance for the leave period. A good deal of leave was spent going about with my mother to see relatives, and I think we all went to the Wood Green Empire, which we found full up, but I managed to get seats in the circle after bribing the doorman (the artful devil). It was marvellous to be back again amonst those I loved and the time went all too soon.

We other ranks had to salute any officer we passed, even in the crowded West End. In Piccadilly I did not bother to salute one officer on the other side of the road, but the military police were everywhere with their beady eyes, and one approached me and threatened to get my leave cancelled for this omission. I felt I could have killed the swine – he had probably never been near a battlefield himself, besides which the West End was teeming with officers. However, my leave was too precious to lose so I had to keep my thoughts to myself.

The time came all too soon to say good-bye, and I left one morning, accompanied by my father who was on his way to the office. I was of course in full marching order with rifle and pack. I left him at Kings Cross and went on to Victoria where I met the rest of my party and entrained for Dover with hundreds of others embarking for Boulogne, marching up to the camp on the hill, spending the night in tents. Incidentally I found that one of the chaps, a corporal, had visited two sisters who lived next door to us at Chesterfield Gardens, while I was out with my mother. I thought this a remarkable coincidence, especially as our regiment was from miles away on the other side of London.

On my first night of leave I found I could not sleep in the unaccustomed soft bed, and like others who had experienced the same difficulty, laid on the floor in a blanket. My mother was so distressed to find me thus the next morning that I used the bed during the remainder of my stay.

After spending the night at Boulogne, we were sorted out for our different destinations and entrained once more for the front. The battalion then were at Laventie, about two miles from the line, my section being billeted on the upper floor of an empty house – quite dry and comfortable. There were still a few civilians in the small town and a few estaminets open.

I often heard mention of a certain Madame Laventie, sometimes known as Madame Bully-Beef, who lived in a little cottage nearby. One of the pioneers named Harry Kay suggested I should go with him to see her. She turned out to be an enormously fat old woman, slumped in a big armchair in the middle of the living room, with two little boys of about four years old, to whom she was acting as foster mother. She apparently was willing to sell us some French beer of which there were several bottles on the table. As she seemed either unwilling or unable to make the effort to raise her great bulk from her chair, we helped ourselves, leaving the money for them on the table.

I never understood why she was such a celebrity, as she seemed quite stupid and made no attempt to converse, just sitting with a contented and smug look on her face. It was quite usual in these villages to find one or two women who acted as foster mothers to youngsters, no doubt deriving their livelihood from this source.

Some of the houses and gardens had been damaged by shell-fire but the sector was very quiet now. We could walk into most occupied houses or cottages in Flanders and get served with coffee (and sometimes cafe-rhum) for a copper or two, and often eggs or omelette and chips. The inhabitants seemed quite poor and only too pleased to make a small profit for themselves. Now and again we got a cigarettte issue or a tin of pipe tobacco. If near an army canteen (which was very rare) we could buy a tin of 50 Woodbines, which were much preferred to the issue cigarettes. In the estaminets we could buy a small Dutch cigar for about 1d. Malaga wine or liqueur was about 2d., also cognac. A bottle (litre) of red or white wine was about 10d. (one franc), so we managed quite well for a few days on our meagre pay of 3s 6d. a week, especially as we were generally paid at intervals of several weeks.

There was of course plenty of card playing and gambling, some fellows staying up nearly all night to play brag or pontoon. I did not join these games, but would sometimes play solo-whist. There were too many experts at pontoon who always seemed to be in funds at the expense of mugs. At times there would be shouts of 'Housey-Housey' and a stampede to the roadside would be made to squat around and play House or what is now known as Bingo. Another game called 'Crown & Anchor' was played with dice on a mat marked off in square symbols. This game was forbidden by the authorities, but the game was often played in some out-of-the-way corner. One could lose money too fast at this racket. Sometimes fellows would play 'pitch and toss' with horse-shoes for quoits. This was a favourite pastime with the Australians. Several games of football were played when opportunity occurred, our battalion being Brigade champions, beating the Rangers, the 4th Londons and the London Scottish. We had a very fine player in Lieutenant Lester, a huge fellow and a university man. I believe he was killed later in the war. He was a very popular officer.

Things soon became too strenuous however for exhausting sports. We served on this now fairly quiet front, 4 days front line, 4 days support line and 4 days in reserve at Laventie. The reserve at Laventie was reckoned as a 'rest' period, but was anything than that. Drills and exercises in the day, ration parties up to the line at night, carrying rations, water, ammunition, duck-boards, barbed wire, etc. Sometimes guard duties in Laventie. This did not allow of much sleep and it was indeed much easier in the line, except for bombing raids, etc. We were worked so hard and kept so busy that we became utterly fed up and began not to care at all what happened to us. Perhaps it was their misguided idea of keeping us on our toes; this policy however having exactly the opposite effect.

During the spring and summer we were mostly engaged in one of the great assaults, but when in reserve we did occasionally lead a fairly tolerable existence if the weather was good, and sometimes even had enjoyable moments.

In winter we were occupied in holding the line and in bad weather would endure much discomfort and boredom, occasionally livened up with patrols and raids, the latter generally causing what seemed to be needless casualties. A simple wound such as a bullet in the thigh could and often did prove fatal during the cold wet nights. These periods were so commonplace as to call for no particular comment. In these relatively quiet periods we were usually able to get some protection from the elements in a flimsy shelter built into the sides of a trench, or even in a small dug-out, and sometimes manage a small coke fire in a perforated oil drum.

In favourable circumstances hot stew and tea could be brought up to the line in dixies or containers, otherwise we subsisted on cold hard-tack and water for several days at a time before being relieved for a few days in reserve.

There were rats in these old dug-outs, very bold and almost tame. I have known one or two venturesome enough to come and take food from our hands if kept perfectly still. They would sometimes sit in their holes staring at us for hours, quickly returning if driven away. Many were covered in mange and some of us contracted a rash on the back of our heads, which I think must have been caused by these ghoulish creatures.

The ground in the line was terribly waterlogged and in fact, as the enemy was on slightly higher ground, their water drained down to our trenches which were impossible in wet weather, being

(*Left*) Sergeant Oborn's cross with the inscription painted by the author. Estaires, 1917. (*Right*) Major Cedric Charles Dickens' cross. He was killed at Leuze Wood on the Somme on 9th September 1916. The author painted the cross and helped to erect it when he was again in the vicinity in 1917.

The Pioneer Section, Arras 1918. *From left to right:* the author, Sweet, Turner, Lance Corporal Greenhill, Maynard, Potter, (at front) Gray, Sparrow. All except Turner and Greenhill were wounded shortly afterwards.

'Gassed', from the painting by John Sargent.

Helping an ambulance through the mud.

completely filled with water. Therefore high barricades or parapets were erected, composed of sandbags – very thick and bullet-proof with wooden revetments and hurdles, fire steps and port-holes for observation, machine guns and snipers. It was very dangerous to expose one's head in daytime, and periscopes were often used for observation purposes.

These high barricades not only allowed walking on comparatively dry duck-boards, but trench shelters were erected in their sides. These shelters or mis-named dug-outs were constructed of timber, sandbags and elephant or corrugated iron, reinforced on top and sides with sandbags. Gas curtains, made of blankets soaked in a chemical solution, were hung at the entrances, with gas-gongs made from brass shell-cases suspended nearby to be struck as warnings in the event of a gas attack or gas-shells. There was occasional rifle or machine-gun fire, but not usually much shell-fire, except from trench mortars and occasional whizz-bangs. The *minnenwerfer* (mine thrower) was perhaps the most hated missile, this being something of the shape and size of an oil drum. This could be seen approaching almost slowly, tumbling over and over in the air and making a terrifying noise, exploding with an enormous eruption. Unless they fell into or on the edge of a trench they would not cause much harm, and if one were smart it was usually possible to judge where they would fall and give one time to dodge round into the next traverse.

The high parapets were useful in this flat territory, as they gave some concealment in getting supplies up to the front line without enemy observation. Indeed in one sector we had a light railway track almost up to the line, on which we could push small laden trucks by hand.

While on the Laventie front a small section of venturesome chaps, known as 'scouts' was formed. They would go over to the German lines at night and getting beyond the front trenches would do whatever mischief they could, once pushing the trucks off an enemy rail track, and so on, with the object of disturbing the Germans' peace of mind and damaging his morale. Occasionally a German would make his way over to our lines at night and give himself up.

One evening a huge sheet of iron was brought into our shelter and I was told to paint the following inscription in large white lettering in German:

The Americans are with us now.
Come over here and we will feed you
    and treat you well.

This was of course untrue at the time, as the Americans were not to arrive in France until a year or so later. However, we fixed this sign above the parapet, but by daylight the Jerries had blown it to smithereens. The message no doubt did something towards lowering their morale. Any prisoner was first interrogated by our colonel before being sent to the rear for further examination. Sometimes they would give useful information as to prospective movements and so on.

Inspired by the constant passing to and fro along the duck-boards, we would sometimes sing:

Have you seen the ducks go by
For their morning walk?
Waddling along they go
As the lanes they roam
There's the Ma duck, the Pa duck,
The Grand Old Drake
Waddling along, what a noise they make,
Have you seen them, have you seen them
Have you seen those ducks go by?

At night one could hear the transport wagons from quite a long distance away as they came up over the hard roads. We could also hear the German transport. It was a period of live and let live, and neither side made a habit of shelling the roads at night. One night however, a shell did fall onto one of our ration parties, causing several casualties, one man being killed, the stretcher bearers going along in daylight to collect the pieces of him in sandbags.

An episode occurred here, which although unpleasant for the recipient, caused much amusement to us. A part of the German trench was open to our view, obviously not suspected by the enemy.

One of our snipers saw some Germans sitting in this trench being served with a meal by a man with a dixie, which he was bending over. Our sniper fired a shot at this fellow's posterior and obtained a direct hit, which laid out the unfortunate man. Our sniper of course made a hasty retreat, as was usual, for the enemy would often locate the rifle fire and would retaliate.

The Germans had many sausage shaped observation balloons, each spaced a few miles apart, just beyond their trenches. We could see two or three of these and would get great entertainment on clear days when one of our aeroplanes would fly over and around one of them, firing incendiary bullets, often bringing the balloon down in flames. The occupants would fling out their papers and descend by parachute. Sometimes an enemy plane would arrive and there would be a dog-fight in the air.

The country here was very flat and almost featureless, a tree or stump here and there and perhaps a bit of a rare hedge or a ditch. There was not much activity beyond a rifle shot now and again, or a short burst of machine gun fire. Sometimes a machine gun would play on one particular part of the parapet or barricade, in an effort to crumble away an opening. An occasional whizz-bang, or trench mortar shell would be fired by either side. At night a flare would be shot into the air from a Very pistol, lighting up the surrounding no-man's-land. If one were out in no-man's-land when this occurred, it was policy to freeze motionless until the light had died down, as any movement would easily be spotted under the flare. A sentry would be posted on the fire step every few yards to keep observation in case of an enemy raiding party or patrol. If any of our men were sent out on patrol a pass-word was to be used to identify themselves on return to the trench. This password would be notified to the troops on each side of the outgoing patrol. The word would be something simple and easily remembered such as 'High Street', 'Tower Bridge' and so on. If the password was forgotten it would probably mean a bullet directed to the absent minded unfortunate.

The powers that be decided on a policy of aggression to constantly harass the enemy and keep the initiative. Frequent bombing raids were carried out at night, fighting and reconnaissance patrols and listening posts sent out into no-man's-land. The fighting patrols were to intercept and attack enemy patrols, the reconnaissance patrols to avoid contact with the enemy, but to bring back information. Wiring parties were also out at night to fix or repair barbed wire entanglements. The listening patrol was often a cold job, lying on the ground generally with an ear close to a bayonet stuck into the earth to act as a conductor of sound.

The bombing raids, led by junior officers, were made with the object of capturing one or more prisoners for future interrogation, or destroying enemy machine guns or emplacements and generally harassing the enemy. Enemy raids on our lines were much less frequent, and I think, wisely so. This policy was very questionable and not worth the very heavy losses sustained. Young lieutenants, many with only a few weeks' experience in the line, were mostly sent on these raids, and we lost a good many of these keen and brave boys and also some of our best and most experienced sergeants and other NCO's, some being caught up and left hanging on the German barbed wire. I remember one young man named Sergeant Oborn, who although wounded, made several attempts to get into the German trench, but was killed on the parapet. Nearly sixty years later a new neighbour of mine at Bembridge showed me a photograph of his brother and one of the cross on his grave at Estaires. I instantly recognised the photograph as that of Sergeant Oborn and also the cross, on which I had painted the inscription. This seemed a remarkable coincidence. This kind of thing seemed a dreadful and callous sacrifice of so many of our finest young men and I am sure the results did not justify the losses. Sergeant Oborn was no doubt endeavouring to take a 'live' prisoner as was the object of the raid. The following letter was sent to his mother by Captain Clarke:

Trenches, B.E.F.

With very deep and personal regret I have to inform you of the death in action of 3302, Sergt. F.S. Oborn, 1/13th. London Regt. He was killed about 3.45 on the morning of the 19th. inst. A raid was in progress and Sergt. Oborn was in charge of the leading party when the raiders were spotted by the German sentries. He charged one of them, was wounded in the chest and staggered back. He charged again and struck the sentry on the head with his rifle, but was again hit in the chest. A third time he charged and was hit in the mouth. He was led back to the centre of no-man's land by a sapper and there collapsed and became unconscious. He was removed on a stretcher but remained unconscious and died before he reached our lines.

He died the best death possible, the death of a fine soldier and a very gallant gentleman. Believe me, I feel his death as an irreplaceable loss to the company and myself. He was the best sergeant I have ever had and I looked forward to the time when he would be an officer in his battalion. Throughout the time I have served with the battalion in trench warfare and on the Somme, his conduct was irreproachable. He was keen, as capable and as forceful an N.C.O. as I have known. In addition he was always cheerful, willing and I valued him as a friend as much as I respected him as an N.C.O. I have recommended him to the Commanding Officer for a posthumous decoration but I do not know whether it will be possible to give it to him.

Please accept my sincere sympathy at his death and believe me, I am as sorrowful at his death as anyone can be who is related to him, but I am very proud that an N.C.O. of my company died so gallantly.

Yours truly,
(sgd) E.F. Clarke,
Captain.

P.S. Sergt. Oborn will be buried in a military cemetery tomorrow with military honours.

Incidentally he did *not* receive a posthumous award.

Some of the raids were carried out in the snowfall, the raiders being dressed in white overalls. We were sent for a short spell to another, but adjacent part of the line, where the trenches and communication trenches were flooded with water and broken ice floating on the surface and thigh deep. We were issued with thigh length wellingtons or waders, for the first and only time. I was unlucky, as they were mostly of small size and none would fit me. This was perhaps just as well, as those who wore them got the boots full of water, making them worse than useless.

One of the companies made a bombing raid in the snow-covered terrain during the night, which turned out to be unsuccessful, and there were a number of casualties. Several of us went out and fetched two of these in. One was unconscious, and was laid out on the firestep, groaning in a mechanical and regular rhythm, awaiting the first aid men. The other man was wounded in the thigh, but died. A thigh wound was often mortal, especially in cold weather.

Four of us took his body back through the flooded communication trench to the road running about 300 yards or so parallel to the front line. We put him on a stretcher and struggled along the trench, over our knees in freezing water, lumps of ice floating on the surface, and into the communication trench, which was similarly flooded. This trench was very narrow and broken down in places, as was some of the front line, where one was exposed to enemy observation and fire. It had by now become daylight and every few yards we had great difficulty in getting round the corners of the traverses, each time having to lift the stretcher over the top of the trench, a very exhausting procedure. It must have taken about two hours to cover this distance. We at last got onto the road by a ruined farm building, dumping the stretcher and its burden in a shed amongst several other corpses.

There was a small dug-out nearby with several of our fellows sheltering round a fire bucket. I got onto a wire bunk, the roof of the dug-out being only a few inches above my head when lying down. The coke fumes were awful and it is a wonder we were not all suffocated. My legs and feet were awfully numb and cold, and although I slapped and punched them it was about six hours before there was any feeling back in them. That evening we fetched the bodies from the shed, where the first aid men had sewn them in blankets, and loaded them on to a transport limber. In the night the rats had eaten their way into the blankets to get at the corpses inside. We were relieved the following evening and gratefully returned to the rear. Incidentally, the troops were issued with whale oil for rubbing into their feet to prevent frost-bite, which became a punishable offence to acquire. I never resorted to the use of whale oil, and it was later discarded as a useless remedy, doing more harm to the feet than good.

On one sector a party of us were billeted in a deserted farmhouse near a cross-road on the La Bassée Road – I think it was called Crucifix Corner or something of the sort, as it had one of the little roadside shrines nearby, so familiar in the Flemish countryside. The road opposite led straight to the front line near Aubers Ridge, about half a mile distant. There was a small ruined orchard at the back and we obtained a felling axe and cut down a few of the apple-tree trunks for fuel. Now and again we found a copper-covered French rifle bullet in the wood. I was chopping up a log on the brick hearth with a long axe, not being used to handling the tool, when it slipped and struck the brick floor, the edge cutting into the sole of my boots between two toes, but without damage to my foot, the brick being hard enough to stop the axe. This made me very cautious when handling a felling axe in the future. As a matter of fact that very week one of our chaps was injured badly in the back by an axe-wielding companion – evidently another novice at the woodman's craft.

There was a brick-walled yard at the front of the house and some of the fellows would take pot shots with their rifles at the rats therein, but as far as I know without success.

Somewhere along the La Bassée Road overlooking the Neuve Chapelle area was a group of buildings and trees, with one brick edifice the upper storey of which was a largish room originally containing a water storage tank. This was now used as an observation post. The fellow in charge invited two of us to go up and look around. There was a small aperture overlooking the battle area across the road and a mile or two of the flat almost featureless countryside rising gently to a low ridge occupied by the German trenches. The no-man's-land seemed very desolated and quiet, with a tree stump or remains of a hedge here and there. We were told that a few of these tree-trunks were actually steel snipers' posts, one in particular being pointed out to us. It was a very convincing imitation of the real thing. It seemed surprising that this small water-tower had not been destroyed by enemy artillery, as it must have been so obvious from the enemy position in the almost featureless countryside, and except for its vulnerability made such an excellent look-out.

This is only one of several instances where seemingly splendid targets were ignored by enemy guns. I suppose there must have been some reason for this, but it is beyond my ken to imagine why. Incidentally it was rather eerie to look over this quiet and seemingly deserted landscape and also be aware that it concealed hundreds of troops, alert and ready to shoot down anyone attempting to traverse its surface, or dangerous even to raise a hand above a parapet.

I am, however, galloping ahead of events, as before the hotted-up period of raids commenced, the division was, to our delight relieved over Christmas for about a fortnight and the battalion marched to Merville, the fair sized town some few miles further back where I had spent such a comparatively pleasant sojourn the year before. We were billeted in large Nissen huts and barns in the Le Grand Pacaut area near the station and the place where I was billeted before.

News of our arrival must have been known beforehand by the inhabitants who lined the roadside to greet us, and we recognised many old friends. Among others was the woman I used to tease by turning out the gas chandelier in her estaminet, and who called out to me as we marched past.

My section was billeted in a comfortable barn or large stable. I took the opportunity of visiting old French acquaintances. These included the old lady and her grandaughter where I was first billeted and who treated me and a companion to a tiny glass of her precious little bottle of home made liqueur. We drew several weeks' back pay and were thus able to make a few visits to the estaminets in the evenings.

The battalion was paraded for inspection by the Brigadier, who reprimanded me for polishing my bayonet with emery paper, thus destroying its original matt surface.

On Christmas day we assembled in the large Nissen huts and seated on benches at long tables. The cooks had excelled themselves by providing a glorious dinner. If I remember rightly this was turkey, but may have been roast beef – I forget now – with Christmas pudding and other good things, served to us by the officers. We were of course in a highly exhilarated state, especially as our football team had beaten the Rangers that morning, to be followed by beating the Fusiliers later in the week by five goals to one, thereby gaining the Brigade cup.

That evening several of us visited estaminets in the town, including the one run by two very prim and reserved young sisters. The place was packed with noisy troops. Among these was a Maltese chap in our battalion, who had recently stabbed another fellow through the hand whilst playing a foolish game of dare, keeping his hand on the table while the Maltese stabbed his jack-knife into the table top. This chap was reputed to be very fiery tempered and dangerous. He was rough-handling one of the two sisters and I got up and told him to stop it as I knew the girls well. He challenged me to a fight, and being rather happy on the white wine and stout laced with champagne (known as black velvet) the two of us with our companions went outside, but waiting for us were two military policemen, who no doubt had been keeping an eye on the estaminet, knowing the girls were running it on their own. We were reprimanded and made to depart in opposite directions. I was probably very lucky, and although we passed each other several days later we did not continue the dispute.

On getting back to the billet the sergeant asked me to call on the regimental police and get them to give us a call in the morning. The police were lying in their blankets up in a barn loft, reached by a ladder. I went up, left my message and turning to the doorway, stepped out into the black night, face forward as if going down a staircase, placed my foot on the top rung of the ladder and immediately pitched over the side onto the muddy cobbles about twelve feet below and thought I had fractured my skull and broken my left wrist. There was a pump in the yard and I put my head under this and doused it with the freezing cold water.

In the morning I had to visit the medical officer who bandaged my badly sprained wrist, put my arm in a sling and said it was a pity I had not fallen a bit harder and broken my wrist which would have meant going back to Blighty. However, the sprain recovered in about a week's time.

While at Merville I also went to the estaminet by the station and saw the other two girls mentioned before, one of whom was dying of TB.

After this enjoyable spell at Merville we went back to the

Laventie sector and the hotted up programme of trench raids, etc.

It was rumoured that the enemy vacated their front line at night time, retiring to their support line owing to our bombing raids, although some rifle and machine gun fire still took place. The tale was that rifles and a machine gun were fixed in their trench and each night a bearded old soldier would go along and pull strings attached to the guns, thus firing them off.

One of our sergeants volunteered to crawl over and try to confirm this rumour, which he did, and got back safely. A raiding party was sent out one night, arrived and found the trench empty, put a fused explosive charge under the machine gun and retired, leaving a lighted fuse wire on the way. Unfortunately one of the raiders coming back from the German trench called out 'Here he comes' and trod on the fuse in his hurry, and that was that.

On another occasion a fighting patrol was sent out in charge of a sergeant, who mysteriously disappeared in the dark. The patrol did come up with an enemy patrol, but both made a hasty retreat from each other. Our chaps got back safely, minus the sergeant, who crept back at dawn saying that he had lost his way and had sheltered in a crater until dawn. The Regimental Sergeant Major, to whom he had to report, gave him the choice of being dealt with by himself or being sent for court martial, which might have resulted in his death by firing squad. He chose the former and the RSM laid him out with a beautiful punch on the jaw, which not only saved the sergeant's life, but also the honour of the regiment.

We heard that a daylight bombing raid, (the first of its kind) had just been successfully made by the Australians. The Kensingtons were ordered to make a second and similar raid to this.

A party of about 150 of us were prepared for this, and a new form of barrage was arranged, known as a 'box barrage', that is heavy shell-fire in the form of a three sided box on the enemy front line trench and on each flank, cutting off any attempt by the enemy of getting round the sides of our raiding party and thus enfilading them. We formed up in our front line and were given a large tot of rum. The inevitable nervous tension and fear of the unknown was somewhat relieved by the feeling of pride that we should have been chosen for this special operation, only the second of its kind in the British Army. An innovation was for a bugler to go over with the party and sound the 'retreat' at the end of the raid.

At about 7 o'clock in the morning after 'stand-to' a heavy barrage began along about 200 yards of German trench, we going over the top and following close behind our barrage, which then lifted on to the enemy second line. The Germans were taken completely by surprise and dived down into their dug-outs, leaving some of their equipment at the entrances, they having apparently just 'stood-down'. We managed to persuade five prisoners up from one dug-out, but in the others the enemy refused to come up, so we pitched grenades down the entrances to finish them off. Some of our party went off to the second line, but found it vacant. Whistles were blown and we returned as rapidly as possible to our own lines, taking the five prisoners with us.

Amazingly the enemy being so surprised and unprepared we all got back without loss, but once in our own trench the Jerries had commenced heavy shelling on the front line and communication trenches, causing us about 30 casualties. The bugler never sounded the 'retreat' as planned. He told me afterwards that he was so nervous that he could not sound a note on his bugle. It was estimated that about 40 Germans were disposed of in addition to the 5 prisoners. High Command were very pleased with the result of this raid and sent congratulations to our battalion.

We had now received large reinforcements, bringing our numbers up to over 30 officers and 1,000 men.

The rest of the brigade were also well reinforced. The London Scottish were particularly lucky, many of their new arrivals being transferred from volunteers from the London police – naturally of good stature, physique and quality.

The Grenadier Guards were staying nearby at the village of Paradis, and I was able to see my cousin Frankie Jones (nicknamed 'Wacky') on several occasions. On going to visit him one cold day, and walking down the completely empty road, there emerged from one of the houses a small and rather fragile looking young officer, his head tucked into the large, turned-up collar of his greatcoat. There was no mistaking him from being Edward, Prince of Wales, and I felt quite a thrill as he returned my salute as we passed. I saw him a couple of times more while in the vicinity. Frankie told me that he sometimes visited the front line, but the Guards of course looked after his safety very well. A newspaper reporter once referred to him as a 'half-baked rabbit', but he did have the courage to go out with a fighting battalion, an experience which no doubt the reporter took good care to avoid.

I remember an embarrassing experience near Merville when we were billeted in an empty semi-detached house, next door being a French family with a very good-looking daughter of about 17. The primitive loo at the end of the garden accommodated both houses, the wooden seats being separated by a partition only 4ft. high. I was seated more or less comfortably when the girl marched down the path, looking straight ahead as if I had not been present and to my consternation entered and seated herself within about 18 inches of me. I was too surprised and embarrassed to move until she had left. The French were much more natural and broad-minded than us. The French soldiers seemed on the whole much more coarse and lewd in front of their women folk, who seemed to take their behaviour as a matter of course.

In contrast to this we once spent a night at a very small and isolated village, the inhabitants all very poor peasants. There was a tiny hall with music emanating from within. Thinking it to be an estaminet I entered a small bare room with a musical machine at one end and a wooden bench along each side. Youths were seated on one side, girls on the other. As each dance tune commenced they got up and met their opposite partners to dance, then returned sedately to their seats. The whole procedure was performed with the utmost solemnity and not a word was spoken. It seemed a most mechanical and boring way of spending an evening, but I suppose in this isolated and barren village it was the only source of entertainment and local etiquette was very strict.

In many parts of Flanders the farms and cottages were very ancient and primitive. Many of the interiors were exactly as depicted by the artists of long ago, such as Teniers and Brouer. A large room with tiled or flagged floor, sometimes even of earth. A large canopied bed at one end, a wooden table with chairs or benches, a large open hearth, or sometimes a round iron stove in the centre of the room, its iron flue going up through the tiled or thatched roof. A very high ceiling with old wooden beams from which hung hams and strings of onions. Sometimes a recess in the wall containing a sleeping place, often of brick and heated from the hearth in some way – a kind of oven I suppose. Very often an elderly man would be seated in a wooden armchair by the fire – morose and brooding, cutting slices of his plug tobacco, often grown from tobacco plants in the garden. He would no doubt be mourning for a son killed at Verdun or the Somme. The women seemed to do all the work on the farm and in the kitchen. They wore long black skirts and usually grey woollen army socks and boots, being mostly far from enticing or romantic. Occasionally a German prisoner would be employed to help on the farm, and would feel very lucky to be engaged in such peaceful, if boring, occupation after the rigours of warfare. Very rarely a young French soldier, invalided from service with severe wounds would be home and working in his fields.

Many of the cottages would be open to us for the sale of coffee, eggs and chips and sometimes rum. The peasants would often prefer a brandy-ball or bullseye with their coffee instead of sugar, which was beet-sugar and not very sweet. Water was nearly always discoloured and polluted and only used for washing, unless boiled for making coffee. It was much too unpalatable and unsafe to drink otherwise, unless chlorinated, which made it taste even worse. The refreshments were very cheap except when Australians, who were much more affluent than us, had previously been in the village, which would cause prices to rise astronomically.

Peculiarly the English and Australians always ignored each other. I do not know the Aussies' point of view, but we were certainly jealous of their affluence and the effect it made on local prices. They seemed to us an undisciplined crowd, with little or no respect for their officers. Our drum and fife band would sometimes play the National Anthem in the evenings, and while we would always stand strictly to attention the Aussies would loll about with hands in pockets. Incidentally it was considered a punishable offence for us to put hands in our pockets or to have a tunic button undone.

The Australians were of course second to none for dash and bravery in the field, and we had great respect for them in this regard. I think they rather looked down on us as Pommies who could not match them as a whole in regard to physique, but did not realise that we had lost the flower of our nation in the early battles of the War, the Somme being the death knell of our fine regiments. The great majority of our troops now were conscripted men, and included many C3 men and those wounded but returned for a further spell of warfare. Except between the few original Kensingtons left, the old esprit de corps was practically non-existent, and even these few of us were now war-weary and consigned to our fate, the war appearing to be a deadlock with little hope of ending before we got our own 'cum-uppence'. The only hope we had was to get a 'blighty one' and return to England on a stretcher.

Take me back to dear old Blighty
Take me back to dear old London Town.
Take me over there, take me anywhere,
Birmingham, Leeds, or Manchester,
I don't care.
I should like to see my best girl,
Cuddling up to me she soon would be.
Carry me back to Blighty,
Tiddly, Iddly Itee,
Blighty is the place for me.

Imagine arriving at a farmhouse, soaked through and tired, glad to get shelter in a cold damp pigsty, about the size of a one-ton coal bunker. We would cram in, several men to a sty, with all our equipment and rifles, lying cramped up in wet uniforms, puttees and boots with legs crossing. Lucky if one managed to get his legs on top of the others. There we would actually sleep, waking in the morning to a rasher of bacon, bread and a pint of tea. Fall in and commence another long march in the rain to our next destination, hoping to be fortunate enough to spend the night in a comfortable dry barn with filthy straw and a horde of rats for company.

At one tiny village, where we stopped for a few hours, a dozen of us were invited into a house for a meal with the very large family of father, mother and a horde of children. This was a very generous gesture, much appreciated by us, as this family seemed very poor in spite of the good spread they arranged for us. This was a great contrast to the behaviour of a young farmer just behind the Somme, who would not let us draw water from his well, but charged us a franc (about 10d) a bucket for it. We also experienced this trouble at another farm.

Water had been so short on the Somme that in one place there was a small tank by the roadside where hundreds of men washed their shirts and socks, besides faces and shaving, the water finally becoming a gluey mess of soap and dirt in the bottom of the tank. The MO issued an order that this tank was not to be used, which was by then too late to be effective.

We passed through many remote villages on our marches to various sectors of the line, most of them being only a cluster of about a dozen or so simple peasants' cottages. I remember one decrepit cottage occupied by an old man in dirty and tattered clothing and was surprised to find that he was dignified by the title of 'Mayor', a certificate verifying this fact was displayed on his living room wall.

Quite often we would come across a woman nursing a baby or young child, and she would tell us that the child was not hers, but that she was only its foster mother or 'wet-nurse'. A favourite lullaby was the song:

Après la guerre finit,
Tous les Anglais partis,
Mademoiselle avec beaucoup de pleuse (picanniny)
Après la guerre finit.

One or two women told us that when the Germans had occupied the village they would hold babies over the fire and burn them. I think we took this tale with a pinch of salt – it was most likely a propaganda stunt.

Some of the villages had a small brewery, and we heard that the Germans had smashed the barrels of beer at one brewery, the beer flowing down the gutters in a stream.

We were sometimes provided quite unconsciously by the villagers with light entertainment, as for instance when the local veterinary surgeon arrived and gelded a young horse on the refuse heap in the middle of the farmyard. The peasants, men, women and children, would stand by solemnly and watch the proceedings, but I must confess that I myself felt rather nauseated by the spectacle. On one or two other occasions it was curious to observe a young woman encouraging and actually assisting a bull in its mating process. This kind of thing was perhaps only to be expected, as in many instances all the able-bodied men were absent from their farms on war service, although the French women on the whole seemed much closer to mother nature and much less inhibited than their English cousins.

At one village, where the chief occupation was the weaving of cloth in a local factory, several of us were billeted for the night on the floor of a front room. This room was devoid of any furniture. In the back room lived a young Frenchman, invalided from the army and his wife, a dark, handsome young woman who worked at the cloth factory, and who had, like many of her neighbours, a large hand loom in the living room. They were an exceedingly nice young couple. The husband was badly crippled by a bullet received at Verdun. His wounds were the most incredible I have ever seen. The bullet had perforated his right forearm, his upper arm, his thigh, his calf and his foot, and he showed us the ten scars to prove it. I would not have believed this possible if I had not actually seen the evidence.

Most of the old men we came across seemed uncommunicative and morose, but a few would talk about '*le sal Boche*' and make a cutting gesture across their throats. After a few drinks they would get into a fiercely patriotic mood and sing '*La Marseillaise*'.

Some of the peasants seemed very primitive in their habits, and once I saw the whole family come out and relieve themselves on a manure heap in front of their cottage before retiring for the night.

There was evidently a good deal of inbreeding in one or two isolated villages, as most of the women in a village would be large, handsome girls with black hair and of very Latin type. In other villages we would see many women with auburn or ginger hair. Very few men would be seen, except for the elderly. Most of the younger men would be in the army or on munition work. The women seemed to do most of the work on the farms. The war must have stretched the manpower of France to the utmost.

I was surprised to find that there was an entire absence of pet dogs in the small towns and villages. There were fierce guard dogs at some of the farms, and these poor animals seemed to be permanently chained to kennels at the farm gates. Others were used to work small treadmills on outside walls, which operated butter churns inside the farmhouses. Dogs would also be harnessed underneath handcarts to help pull the vehicles along the streets. Neither do I recall seeing a pet cat. It seems no wonder that the country was running alive with rats. There must have been a few cats about. The only one I remember was living wild in a small bomb-shelter dug into the side of a communication trench near Laventie. It had made its home amongst the wooden boxes of hand grenades. I tried to befriend it, but it rushed away scared and swam rapidly along the flooded trench bottom, beneath the duck boards, and into a sump, the sides of which were too steep and slippery for it to climb out. I tried to extricate it, but had my hands scratched and bitten badly by the frantic spitting and swearing animal, so had to leave it to its own devices.

I would like to tell you now of a weird experience I had on the Laventie front. One evening five of us were detailed as a carrying party to fetch some reels of barbed wire from an engineers' dump on the road running behind and parallel to the trenches. This was at the end of a communication trench, the top of which was about six feet high. Darkness had fallen and we were standing talking at the roadside. A section of the front line trench had been left unmanned for about 40 yards, as it was believed to have been mined by the enemy.

Suddenly our conversation stopped and everything was still and silent. The figure of a tall man passed along the top of the trench. He was about five yards distant, striding steadily and as if absorbed in thought, towards the rear area where stood a derelict farm house. The figure appeared as a solid dark silhouette against the lighter night sky. It seemed to be dressed in a German type field uniform and round field service cap, and was not carrying equipment or rifle. Peculiarly enough there was no sound of his progress, which was unlikely on the rough ground.

The incident could have only taken about half a minute or less. The sensation felt was extraordinarily uncanny and I was quite certain that the figure was that of a phantom, although it appeared opaque. I was momentarily frozen and incapable of action, although there was no question of fear; we were all armed and experienced men. After it had passed our conversation was resumed. I felt too awed and embarrassed to mention the subject to my companions, although I was certain they also had seen the same thing but did not care to mention it. The episode was, as usual, soon forgotten. When passing the farm some time afterwards a fellow in another company told me that earlier in the War a German spy used to get over our lines and visit collaborators at this farm to pass information, but was eventually caught and shot. I did not tell this fellow of my experience with the phantom.

The place where I had the near accident with an axe was alongside the La Bassée Road. This road was parallel to and about a half mile distant from the German line, and being in very flat country was under observation in the daytime. One evening I was sent to meet a young storeman from the quartermaster's store in Laventie at a point about a quarter mile distant along this road, where one of our light rail tracks ended. He was a rather brazen and showy young fellow, evidently thrilled by probably his first visit to the line. As we walked along he lit a cigarette, ignoring my warning that the light could be seen from the enemy trenches. Suddenly 'zipp', a sniper's bullet just missed us and he dropped his cigarette hurriedly and said not a word for the rest of our journey.

In those days we were not trained so strictly as in the last War in the necessity for concealment and track discipline, being left to learn by experience often too late.

Apropos to this, I remember being billeted in an old farm building alongside a similar road at Foncquevillers, near Hebuterne. Part of this road was screened by very high camouflaged netting on tall poles. Being curious I ventured a short distance on the enemy side of the netting and stood looking around. Suddenly four shells whizzed over and exploded about thirty yards short of me. I was obviously observed and so walked back to the barn. I remember thinking, 'That must have cost the Jerries a £100 or so.' How ignorant and careless of danger some of us were in those days.

Shortly before leaving Laventie it was rumoured that a battalion of New Zealand Maoris was to share our billets. This caused us much consternation, as we did not relish the idea of living in close proximity with what we thought were primitive and uncouth savages. As a matter of fact they were actually billeted in another part of the village. I went into an estaminet one day and there were about a half-dozen of these Maoris in there. I sat at a table near them and was amazed to find them all talking together in impeccable English accents, evidently well educated and cultured. They were all tall, of fine physique and smartly dressed in their khaki uniforms. They were remarkably handsome of feature. I do not know if these fellows were something special, or if typical of the Maori race. As I was never in contact with New Zealand troops again I did not get the opportunity to find out. Anyway, I felt that I would be proud to be in their company.

It was early in March 1917 when we left the Laventie area for the Arras front. When on long marches the senior officers were mounted on horses, the Colonel, Major, Adjutant, Quarter Master and Medical Officer, and also the four Company Commanders or Captains, the latter on horses borrowed from Brigade. One young officer was never able to control his mount, which would sometimes run away with him and had to be caught by the transport corporals. This would cause much merriment to us less fortunate foot-sloggers. The MO would ride at the rear and force on those unfortunates who had fallen out, sometimes with the threat of his revolver. I remember mentioning this to an elderly doctor on the medical board at the end of the War. He seemed deeply shocked and would not believe me.

We were relieved by a Yorkshire regiment, and spent our nights en route at various villages and towns, mostly by marching, but by train from Merville to Doullens and Ivergny where we endured a session of hard training in muddy fields. At one village the local farmer had in some way annoyed our Brigadier General, who after Church Parade made our battalion march and drill backwards and forwards over his immaculately ploughed field. This punished us as much as the farmer, for the going was very hard in the trampled and muddy furrows. This foolish action was typical of some of the old die-hard officers, and hardly contributed to the War effort.

The battalion was now up to full strength and properly organised once more. The medium machine gunners (Vickers Gun) were now detached and formed into a separate company under control of

Brigade. The Lewis guns, one to each platoon with its team, the Stokes Mortar sections, bombers and their bayonet men carrying extra satchels of grenades, the rifle grenade men with rifles fitted with cups at the muzzle and the barrels reinforced with wire, the marksmen or snipers, the stretcher bearers largely composed of the men from our old brass band, the Company Quarter Masters and their storemen. Each officer had his own servant, the Regimental Sergeant Major his batman, the Head Quarter and Company runners, the signallers, and so on, nearly all men falling into one or other of these categories.

We heard rumours that we were soon to take part in another big attack at Arras. We old soldiers did not relish this prospect very much, especially after our terrible experiences of the Somme.

However at Ivergny a battalion sports day was organised and was enjoyed immensely. The transport provided a mock general, red tabs and all, riding a horse and accompanied by two fellows dressed as girls. Passing the guard house, the sentry suddenly confronted with this spectacle and seeing the red tabs, presented arms and turned out the guard. There were the usual running, jumping, tug-of-war and other competitions, the transport giving a very creditable display of horse riding, cowboy fashion, one or two riders even leaning down from the saddle and picking up handkerchiefs in their mouths from the ground.

I think it was here that we were to be inspected by a very high ranking general (it may have been Haig). Our Colonel had the brilliant idea of outshining the other participating battalions by painting our steel helmets a khaki colour complete with the red diamond patches on the sides. A large quantity of brown and scarlet paint was conjured up from the engineers, together with brushes, and details of men were set to work on the job. The wet helmets were then passed on to the Pioneer section to paint the red diamonds. I cut out some stencils and we got to work on the almost impossible task of completing it before daybreak. There were no thinners for the paint and one of the officers used paraffin oil for the purpose, the result of course being that the paint would not dry. The hundreds of steel helmets were laid out in the field to try and dry them. Harry Kay volunteered to keep the farmer's chicken from roosting on the tops. Armed with a pile of stones his aim was too true and he accidentally knocked one of the birds out. We had chicken for supper that evening after hurriedly plucking and disposing of the feathers before the farmer started investigations.

Needless to say there was much grousing when the troops collected their sticky wet helmets, which soon became messed up and smudged, to say nothing of hands and uniforms. To add to the indignity the inspecting general severely reprimanded our Colonel and ordered the removal of the paint by rubbing it off with mud. Our sleepless night's work had been in vain and the air was thick with blasphemy.

V

Total Dedication – Spanners in the Works

We marched from here towards Arras, stopping at a small village for the night. It began raining very heavily at mid-day and when we had become thoroughly soaked through the order came to don our groundsheet capes, which were by then quite useless. I had to sleep with others packed on the sloping cobblestones under the archway to a farmyard. The water was pouring down the cobbles in a stream.

It was still pouring the next morning when we resumed our march to Arras. On our way we could hear the heavy gunfire increasing in loudness as we got nearer. After the nice rest period we had recently enjoyed we felt a bit queazy at the thought of going into action again. The longer one survived the more windy one felt of going up to the line again. Luck could not last for ever, although we would joke that 'they haven't put our name on one yet'. Peculiarly this feeling would pass off once we had arrived, so long as we could keep fairly active. It might be mentioned here that dug-out life could have a rather demoralizing effect, and no doubt this was one reason that our Higher Command did not construct many deep dug-outs as did the Germans. Also our policy seemed to be one of constant aggression, whereas the Germans concentrated more on very strong defensive positions such as the Hindenburg Line with its concrete pill-boxes, exceedingly deep and often immense dug-outs and broad bands of barbed wire which in places were probably forty yards in width and had to be destroyed or pierced by heavy artillery fire and other means to permit a successful attack.

We arrived at Arras in the afternoon and marched through the town which showed surprisingly little damage considering that it had been occupied in turn by the Germans, French and British. The worst damage seemed to be to the railway station, which was a ruin and also the Cathedral.

We soon found, however, that many of the houses were a shambles inside. There were still a few civilians about and some estaminets open, but mostly in the part of the city furthest from the line. Many of the houses on the extreme outskirts had been shelled and ruined, and it seemed to us then peculiar to see houses with walls blown down and the bedrooms still fully furnished and exposed to view. Nowadays of course this had become a familiar sight during the aerial bombings of the last war.

We were ensconced in the Schramm Barracks with its large empty rooms overlooking a central cobbled court yard. Here we drew blankets and stripped off our sodden clothing which we hung about in an endeavour to dry it off as much as possible. Some were lucky enough to take advantage of the large warm cook house, where our cooks had managed to light up the fires and ovens.

Next day the sun came out and we found a small pond outside the further gate. Many of the chaps, including myself, jumped in for a swim. The water was filthy and full of old iron and other refuse, draining the road as it did. However, we managed a bit of a swim before the MO put it out of bounds on hygienic grounds.

We then marched off a couple of miles or so to the suburb of Achicourt, the route being lined with houses. This village was surrounded by fields, a number of women working on the crops. It contained a large square with the Mairie at one end, and seemed peaceful enough at the time, and most of the houses were still occupied by civilians, although only a mile or so from the front line at Beaurains. Its peace, however, was soon to be shattered as I will relate.

The battalion was dispersed to various huts and buildings, my section going to the cellar of a small house in the square, close to the Mairie. There were one or two tiny shops with nothing but a very few goods for sale, such as bread, tobacco, chocolate meunier and the usual centre piece of very old, dry and fly-blown ginger cake.

Batteries of artillery guns, some of huge calibre, and lorries of ammunition were passing through the village, and also a contingent of cavalry.

The next evening we started off towards Beaurains, our section going through the small gardens between two cottages and coming out onto a road, crossing a bridge over a deep railway cutting, now to be used as battalion headquarters. We found Beaurains to be a small village surrounded by trees and perched on a ridge overlooking a wide expanse of plain falling gently towards another village called Neuville Vitasse, a mile or so away and occupied by the Germans. Beaurains was to have been attacked the week before by the Rangers, but had been evacuated by the enemy who had now taken up a heavily wired trench in front of Neuville Vitasse. I mistook this wire as a long narrow field, rusty brown until told what it really was. Heavy barrages were put down on this broad belt of barbed wire to try and smash it up, but not very successfully.

An officer and a party of men went over no-man's-land at night with a few bangalore torpedoes, a section of what seemed iron drain pipe which was full of explosive, to cut three lanes through the wire. I carried one of these torpedoes forward and it was placed in position and detonated by chaps trained for the job. These devices proved very successful. The job was carried out without loss and apparently undetected by the enemy. We also moved down one night into the valley and dug an assembly or assault trench nearer the enemy line.

Owing to heavy rain the impending attack was postponed and we moved back to Achicourt for a few days. Moving up to Beaurains once more my company took up a position in support on the ridge and just to the right of the road which ran straight ahead to Neuville Vitasse. We crossed the road past a small but high brick wall and into a shallow trench which was little more than a ditch. We were soon moved forward to what must have been a strongpoint, being a series of trenches roughly in the shape of a square, and just over the top of the ridge. This position afforded a fine view of the sloping ground leading down to Neuville Vitasse, but very exposed to observation from the German lines. Over to the left and slightly behind we could see some buildings, obviously the railway station and some tile factories on the outskirts of Arras and some more buildings a mile or two on the right. Immediately in front was Neuville Vitasse, with its many now ruined red brick houses and trees, showing up quite clearly, the long brown field of rusty barbed wire running in front of the village.

There was an immense concentration of artillery guns in the country behind the lines, and more still coming up from the rear areas. These were of all calibres, 18 pounder field guns, 6-inch howitzers and heavier, and also to our surprise some 16-inch naval guns – throwing an immense armour piercing shell. We had never seen so many, even on the Somme, and it was said that if in a single line they would have been wheel-to-wheel. There were thousands of them for miles along the front to be attacked. There were also great ammunition dumps, with every kind of shell stacked high, often with the barricades of earth between stacks, each dump appearing to cover acres of ground. It was amazing to think of the colossal effort our country and America must have made to manufacture and ship this great arsenal.

During the afternoon – it was Easter Sunday 1917 – there suddenly erupted the most terrific barrage on and over the enemy lines that I had ever experienced and would never before have thought possible. Thousands of guns were firing hundreds of thousands of shells. The din was terrible and unbelievable, like a hundred thunderstorms rolled into one, going on without pause for an hour or two. Besides the explosions of the guns and the detonations of the shell bursts one could hear the train-like roar of the heavy shells and the shriek and whistle of the smaller calibres as they passed overhead.

The sight that met our eyes was even more amazing, the German lines and the village being covered with the smoke of the exploding shells. Houses and trees were rapidly being demolished and it seemed impossible that anybody could remain alive in that hell. The shell bursts were mostly white clouds of smoke, some black, and wherever a brick building was hit the brickdust coloured the smoke red. It was marvellous to know that we were now getting some of our own back. We were so exhilarated that most of us were jumping up and down with excitement. I did not notice any retaliation from the enemy artillery, and our tremendous barrage must have silenced their own guns and no doubt destroyed many.

A party from headquarters, including the brigadier himself,

came and stood on the ridge observing the barrage. They stayed in the open until things had quietened down again, when suddenly a dozen or so shrapnel shells burst overhead, and a few sniper's bullets passed too close for their liking and they disappeared quickly to their dug-outs well to the rear. In spite of the holocaust some at least of the enemy had managed to survive in their shelters, to pop up as soon as the barrage ceased.

Remembering that it was Easter Sunday, I wondered what my parents and sister were doing on that day, and what their thoughts would have been if they had known what was going on around me.

Later in the afternoon there was a slight fall of snow. What we had experienced on that afternoon, exhilarating as it had been, gave one the uncomfortable and awesome feeling that man had challenged and even surpassed the Almighty in creating the ultimate horror of violence and destruction in so short a period. It must of course be remembered that the atom bomb had not then even been thought of.

We were to attack Neuville Vitasse soon after dawn on the morrow, Easter Monday, 9th April 1917. Aware now that we would get strong artillery support and being well briefed in regard to our plan of action and the objectives to be aimed at, we felt much more confident than during the Somme battles, where we were nearly always engaged in muddle and inefficiency from the top downwards. It appeared that Higher Command had learned a great deal from the former battles and could now plan out the various stages of assault in a more thorough and efficient manner.

The scientists had discovered much more accurate ways of spotting and ranging on enemy gun positions from far back and even up to and including the forward machine gun emplacements. What was perhaps equally important was improvement of the means of communication, a primitive type of wireless having been adopted, which together with field telephones, telegraphy, runners, signallers and even pigeon carriers had made contact between companies, battalion and brigade much more efficient.

There were miles of good roads behind the lines and many engineers, labour battalions and even Chinese, were incessantly at work laying and repairing miles of wooden sleeper tracks from the roads and up as far as possible to the battle area. These heavy wooden sleepers were found to be superior to rubble or hardcore, floating on top of the mud instead of sinking down into quagmires and shell holes. These roads and tracks enabled motor driven lorries to come nearer the battle area, thus getting supplies and shells up more quickly and efficiently and also permitting the use of motor ambulances from advanced aid posts and dressing stations. The wounded, however, still had long and arduous journeys before arriving at pick-up stations.

We moved up to the assembly positions during the night, received a good issue of rum and waited for zero hour. The wait before zero hour was a most miserable and nerveracking experience, and in spite of the rum the suspense gave one an awful feeling as of a cold stone in the pit of the stomach. The barrage ahead started with a terrific roar and it was obviously tearing the German positions apart. This helped to put a little more hope and confidence in my mind.

The Rangers were on our left; all our four companies were to go forward straight through the barbed wire and enemy front line and through the village – two companies leading and two companies (including my own) following up, both in four lines. I was in the second line of B Company. Four tanks were to go into action with us, but again either did not get started or were soon stopped.

Before our zero-hour we learned that the Canadians had by now stormed and taken the formidable Vimy Ridge on the extreme left and soon after an English division had over-run Telegraph Hill on the immediate left of Neuville Vitasse, thus covering our left flank. Whistles shrilled along our trench and as we clambered out and lurched forward, bayonets fixed, the movement seemed to ease the tension. The inactivity of the waiting period was the most trying. A heavy creeping barrage fell on the enemy front-line to which we advanced as closely as possible behind the barrage, which then lifted onto the village, we following as each stage of the barrage lifted further forward. This time the artillery performed perfectly. There was little difficulty in getting through the gaps in the smashed up wire.

In spite of the barrage we were faced with a considerable amount of machine gun fire, but the shell fire was much less than we had expected, owing to the good work of our own artillery in keeping the enemy batteries subdued. I was not unduly worried by machine gun fire or by the shrapnel overhead. It was the high explosive shells that were most terrifying, screaming down and bursting, throwing up great geyzers of earth and smoke, filling the air with acrid fumes. It was a matter of following the extended line ahead and trying to keep in touch with the chaps on one's right and left. There was neither time nor inclination to observe what was going on around. A man would fall or disappear here and there. If a man nearby was hit we were not allowed to stop and help him – our job was to go on to our objectives without diversion, and indeed our main wish was to get out of this open ground and into some sort of cover from missiles as soon as possible. A shell burst just ahead on my right and a man fell on his back, his head turned to one side, his face and shoulder a horrible red mess.

My mind was of course concentrated on what was immediately around me, but I saw several men pitch forward as they were hit. Nearing the German front trench I felt a jerk at my right hip and thought I had been hit, and jumping into the demolished trench saw the bodies of several Germans, and a couple with their hands up in surrender. They looked terribly shaken – one was quite a young boy. They were at once sent towards the rear, where they would be taken over by the 4th Londons who were in support, the London Scottish being in reserve.

I felt something cold running down my right leg and looked down expecting to see blood, but discovered that a bullet had pierced my water bottle near the top, spilling water down my thigh. We moved forward as the barrage lifted and got amongst the remains of houses and gardens at the left of the village, passing the bodies of a few men, both ours and the Germans, and some wounded and prisoners making their way to the rear. Those wounded unable to get up, we had to leave for the stretcher bearers to deal with later, as we had strict orders not to stop our advance – the normal instructions being 'Every man for himself'.

Scrambling through the smashed and ruined buildings, over shell holes, brick rubble and broken timbers, we reached our final objective known as Moss Trench at the far side of the village where we scraped and dug what cover we could in this now shallow ditch. A considerable amount of machine gun fire and rifle grenade fire coming from what we knew to be part of the Hindenburg Line known as the Cojeul Switch, a short distance to our front. This caused us a number of casualties.

We learned that the Rangers had also got through and contacted us on our left. However, our right flank was exposed as the Middlesex had been held up and a party, including Lewis gunners and bombers formed a short line on this flank to give covering fire to the Middlesex. There was an enemy strong point several hundred yards to the right at Neuville Mill. The Tanks managed to get through there and soon gave valuable assistance in overcoming this obstacle. Before mid-day it was reported that all objectives had been gained, and the London Scottish passed through us and attacked and took the Cojeul Switch, passing on to their final objective towards Wancourt.

The Kensingtons' losses we learned later had been about 130 including 6 officers and we had captured 100 prisoners, 6 machine guns, 2 heavy and 3 light mortars. We were to relieve the London Scottish later in the day, but some of us were detailed to escort prisoners to the rear. Many of these were employed as stretcher bearers, some even volunteering for the job. The RSM told me to report to the Pioneer Section, as I would be wanted to paint inscriptions on some of the captured mortars. I found the section sheltering in what was left of a German dug-out beside ruined buildings on the roadside through the village. There was a corporal and six or seven men, all of which I knew well from previous contacts with the pioneer section at Hebuterne. That evening the Sergeant arrived and took us back to Achicourt.

Something terrible had happened here. We entered Achicourt this time at a different point, going along a road running parallel to and between the main Arras Road and the railway line. It was dark when we arrived and passed the small working class houses, most of which were in ruins and smoking, the interiors looking like red hot firegrates. Small groups of frightened men and women were still hurrying away with hand trucks and perambulators filled with whatever of their simple belongings they had been able to salve from their destroyed homes. At the end of the road we emerged on the square which was a litter of destruction. One row of houses, about 6 or 8, bordering the square were in ruins. A whole platoon of about 30 or so Queen's Westminsters had been billeted in these and were all killed. We tried to explore them the next day, but they were in too dangerous a condition, ceilings and roofs due to collapse at any minute and staircases smashed.

The Mairie had suffered some damage from shell fire but was still standing, and I found the cellar where I was billeted a few days before in the corner of the square to be quite undamaged and we settled in there for the night. In the morning we visited the transport section, about 400 yards distant in a pleasant field, and learned what had happened. It appears that on Easter Sunday a convoy of about 20 motor lorries, containing shells, had been parked in the square. These had been spotted by a German airman and reported to his artillery who sent over salvos of shells, their fire being directed from above by the airman, destroying many houses and exploding a load of huge 9-inch shells on one of the lorries, setting fire to other vehicles.

Some of our transport personnel went to do what they could to help extinguish the fires on the lorries under the direction of Major Campbell who was in the village at the time. They drove some of the lorries away out of danger, some to a pond just outside the village, and managed to quench those on fire. One of the corporals received the DCM for this and another man (I think the wheelwright) got a Military Medal. Great pieces of shell and ironwork were blown as far away as the transport lines, over a quarter of a mile distant. Many of the civilians were not rescued from their ruined homes until hours afterwards and their losses must have been great.

I managed to get two small tins of Ripolin enamel, black and white, from the stores. I had fortunately got a small goose-quill lettering brush in my pocket book, so was now equipped for the job to which I had been delegated, that is, to paint inscriptions on the mortars and machine guns recently captured and some of which were sent home to be displayed in our drill hall in Kensington. I also took the opportunity to get a replacement for my water-bottle.

We went back to Neuville Vitasse that afternoon and found a part demolished German dug-out in what had been a garden close to a ruined house. We were lucky as all other shelters appeared to have been smashed in by shellfire. The roof was only about 2ft. thick, sloping dangerously. It was pitch dark inside. We lit candle ends and saw a bare space with shelves on one side, still containing some of the unpalatable black bread issued to the Germans. We were not tempted to sample this. The dug-out stank with the sharp and unpleasant odour peculiar to these German dug-outs, no doubt due to the effects of their black bread and other food. The smell was quite distinct from that of the British. There had been some drizzle and sleet, so we were grateful to get even this shelter for the night.

Next morning we looked around the ruins, finding the remains of what had been the Town Hall or Mairie. There were several huge unexploded 16-inch naval shells lying nearby, which owing to their low trajectory had no doubt slid on their sides along the ground instead of falling nose down and detonating. Rude messages had been chalked on one of them by some wit.

Also in a battered trench I found a most curious German rifle, the metal parts being bright and silvery – no doubt chromium plated. It must have been some regimental trophy, as the brilliant silver colour would have shown up too much for it to have been of any practical use. I would have liked this as a souvenir, which was of course out of the question owing to its cumbersome size and weight. We had more than enough to carry as it was. I did, however, remove the bolt which I slipped into my pocket, but had to discard it later for convenience sake.

We were soon instructed to take some 2 gallon petrol cans filled with water up to the battalion, who were by now advanced to a position several hundreds of yards beyond the Hindenburg Line and near the village of Wancourt, this village still being in German hands. On the way we saw a dead German by the roadside, still wearing a gold ring on one of his fingers. One of the fellows tried to remove the ring but could not get it off the now stiffened finger.

Just beyond Neuville Vitasse we crossed the part of the Hindenburg Line recently taken by the London Scottish. This was built up behind a very wide and deep trench, a kind of moat, intended to prevent the passage of tanks. An immense amount of concrete and steel had been used in this system, with many strong pill-boxes and other structures slotted for machine guns, trench mortars and other weapons. There was a marvellous system of very deep dug-outs having about 50 steps down to long galleries with underground rooms, some capable of containing a hundred or more troops, with first aid rooms, officers' quarters, kitchens and all kinds of amenities. Many of these galleries had about six entrances, ensuring exit and ventilation in the event of one or more entrances being blown in. The Germans had evidently expected a very long stay in this line.

Beyond this we proceeded over open ground to a ridge before Wancourt, passing a damaged and deserted tank. There was a pile of machine gun ammunition on the ground in a shell hole immediately below the door, where the team or following troops had been using their Lewis gun. Wherever the tanks had been engaged we would see many very small calibre bright steel shells with pointed noses, which no doubt were armour piercing shells of naval type used by the tanks. There was no sign of life around this open countryside which was quite featureless. The ground was torn up and pitted with shell-holes, but nothing like what we had been used to on the Somme, where every yard of ground was fought over stubbornly backwards and forwards until finally overcome.

The Germans had now learned to retire to well prepared positions when hard pressed, and except for valuable strong-points and positions not to engage in fruitless slog-outs. They must have been feeling the heavy losses sustained on the Somme and at Verdun in addition to those on the Russian front. There seemed a good proportion of men of advanced middle age as well as youngsters, many looking no more than 17 years of age, and of questionable physique. Their best regiments, however, were composed of very sturdy specimens and splendidly disciplined and formidable.

After delivering our loads of water to the various QM positions, we returned to Neuville Vitasse. The German body we had passed on the way up was now minus not only the gold ring, but the finger also. Someone not so squeamish as us had been at work.

When we got to our overnight dug-out we found that it had now collapsed, the flat roof having fallen in. We realized how lucky we had been. As we stood looking at this a rifle was fired from somewhere amongst the ruins, the bullet passing quite close. The ground here was so broken up and littered with collapsed buildings

Back home again.
The author and his father,
September 1918.

In the Stoke War Hospital, Newcastle-under-Lyne, June 1918. The author is on a stretcher in the front row.

Back in Civvy Street.

and debris that there was little chance of finding the sniper and it was not possible to determine the exact position from which the shot had been fired, so we shifted to a spot further along. A strange event, but it may have been a wounded German who had been overlooked or had hidden away from the mopping-up parties.

The sergeant arrived and showed us where two of the mortars were positioned in a firing pit – one large *minnenwerfer* and one smaller mortar. These were the only two to be inscribed and I was given a piece of paper with the requisite wording, as far as I remember 'Captured at Arras 9th April 1917 by the Kensingtons, 13th. London Regt.' I painted these words in white Ripolin on each weapon, joined the other chaps and we searched for another place to settle down.

This kind of more-or-less easy going life was much better than being with the company. We got on very well together, did what we wanted and wandered about at will so long as there was no job to do. No strict discipline or exercises, no guard or sentry duties, and no stand-to morning and evening unless we were engaged in the front line, which was not often. The sergeant we seldom saw, as he was mostly back in the transport lines or HQ stores with other details such as the Tailor, Shoemaker, Orderly Room Sergeant and so on. As far as we could tell they did nothing much but eat, drink and play cards.

Our corporal, who was always with us, was a pleasant, good-natured free and easy fellow. We all addressed him as Charlie. He was a finely built and strong young man, and although so chummy could, if necessary, be very tough. On two occasions I saw him lift a man up at arm's length above his head and throw him to the ground. Incidentally I saw him in the Kensington Drill Hall after the Second World War. He was serving as Canteen Sergeant, and had been out again to France, being made prisoner at Dunkerque, spending the rest of that war in a German prisoner of war camp.

We got our share of hard work and danger when up the line, so had the satisfaction that we were engaged in useful work in the battle area. The freedom from strict routine gave us a splendid opportunity to observe what was going on both in and behind the front line and how the work of the various units linked up – the infantry, transports, supply of food and ammunition, the tasks of the artillery and engineers and so on. In fact, how the great machine ticked over. Many a time after getting food, water and ammunition to the front, over miles of deep mud and shell-holes, during the night as well as daytime, often through heavy shell fire, I felt great satisfaction in getting the job completed successfully and on time. We never let conditions or danger hold us up, even for a short time.

It seems a curious thing, but sometimes a man coming down from the line on some errand or other would say that he preferred the trenches to our usually exposed position in open ground, and would hurry back to the line as quickly as he could. We seldom got much danger from rifle or machine gun fire, but were very exposed to shell fire from the heavier guns, searching the ground for our artillery positions, tracks and road junctions. Many chaps thought we had a cushy time as Headquarters details, and so we did in some respects, although such details as regimental police, drummers, signallers and pioneers sustained considerable losses. For instance our regimental police numbering about 8 men at a time, lost in all 2 sergeants and 5 men killed and 3 or 4 wounded. Our drummers, I suppose about a dozen strong, had several men killed and quite a few wounded. Our pioneer section, normally about 8 strong, eventually lost 6 men (myself included). It was therefore not so cushy a job after all. This also applied to other regiments, the Fusiliers for instance having many of their pioneers killed or wounded.

Sustained shell-fire was the most trying and terrifying thing to be feared by all. Many of us were naturally prepared to face up to rifle or even machine gun fire without much trepidation, as one felt there was a sort of sporting chance, and even an opportunity to hit back, as also with hand grenades. Shell-fire, however, was something devilish and beyond comprehension. There was no chance at all to take reasonable shelter from the horrifying effect of a direct or a near hit even if in a dug-out where one could be buried alive, and even by a trench wall.

The really brave man is one who knows fear; but is able to conquer it. I have known some men who have crouched under close shell-fire with their teeth chattering uncontrollably like castanets, and staring in front of them with white faces, eyes opened wide with fright. The fellows would, however, manage to control their fear once they got active. We all felt terrible fear at times, even the bravest, but the thing was to try not to show this and so spread fear to others. There were on occasion cases where a man's reason broke down and he had to be sent back with shell-shock. I remember seeing one particular sergeant whose bravery had always been admired, but who eventually broke down with shell-shock, weeping uncontrollably on his way back to the dressing station.

However, to get back to my narrative, the next morning we were sent on a mission to the top of Telegraph Hill on the left of Neuville Vitasse; this hill had been captured a few days previously. The eight of us set off over open ground and ascended the hill, shaped like a huge pimple. At the top was a large circular space of thick concrete, evidently used once by the Germans as the base for a large gun. There were a couple of coffin shaped shelters, mere concrete slits about 6 feet long and 2ft. 6 ins. wide and roofed with concrete. There was just enough room in the one which Dick Sweet and I got into. Dick squeezed into a small hollowed out ledge and I crouched on the floor for the night. The entrance of course faced the wrong way, being exposed to enemy fire.

In daylight there was a marvellous view from this position over the valley and plain towards Arras itself. One could see for miles around; it must have been a wonderful and commanding position for the Germans, both for observation and defence. On the enemy side of the crest, about 50 yards or so away, was the most intriguing trench system I had yet encountered, and commanding the whole of the top of the hill, with a clear field of fire against unsuspecting troops attacking over the opposite crest. These trenches were well protected by concrete embrasures. The tops of all trenches and approach or communication trenches leading down the hill at the rear, were covered completely. Very little damage had been done to them by shell-fire. We explored the front trench which was well fitted up with cubby holes and resting places, and must have been very comfortable for the former occupants. The passages or tunnels leading to the rear were pitch dark and we did not feel at all inclined to venture into them without a light, so went back to our concreted position. We did not explore over the tops of these trenches, as no doubt we would have made splendid targets, although there must have been a very interesting view over the country towards Monchy and Wancourt.

Towards evening it was pretty obvious that we had been spotted by the Germans, as salvos of heavy shells arrived on our position, causing us to crouch in our shelters. This shelling went on for most of the night and put the fear of hell into us, so accurate was the ranging. However, by dawn the firing ceased and all was quiet. It seemed evident that the only reason we had been sent here was for Division Headquarters to see if we would be spotted as they were no doubt considering the possibility of utilizing the hill for observation or other purposes. I don't think it was ever used, being too exposed and dangerous. We had once more been used as live bait. The Regimental Sergeant Major himself arrived alone in the morning and led us down the steep hillside to the plain below, on the way to Arras. As we were crossing an old trench half a dozen shrapnel shells exploded just above our heads, the nose caps making that nasty whirring sound as they sped down. Shrapnel did not worry me to any great extent as did high explosive. If directly overhead the chance of being hit was not great, as the bulk of the shrapnel was sprayed forward, although the steel shell-case often did not disintegrate, but came down intact. The nose cap was particularly dangerous hurtling down with a vicious whirr, and was capable of decapitating a man.

We stood on the parapet of the old trench, but the Sergeant Major told us to get down, but he himself stood up on top until the shelling stopped. Being an old guardsman, I believe he took a pride in showing defiance and in setting an example to his men. He would, however, strongly reprimand anyone, including officers, for showing the slightest fear or ducking under fire. In the old days any flinching from danger was considered a disgrace. In the last war much more common sense was used, and concealment and evasion from unnecessary exposure to danger was taught and encouraged. After all, a live soldier was more useful than a dead one. We were on the whole very naïve in respect of concealment, taking it for granted that if we were not actually in the line we were free from observation, which of course was a fallacy. The art of concealment and track discipline was not taught, as it is nowadays and practised in the Second World War.

However, looking back to the event, I am certain that this route was deliberately chosen as part of our task to discover whether the area was under enemy observation. The surrounding ground as far as we could see was deserted and not even containing artillery positions. The Germans must have had pin-point ranging of the area, and waited until we were actually on the trench before opening fire, hence the accuracy of the shell-fire. We were fortunate that high explosive shells were not used, otherwise we would have been obliterated.

We arrived in Arras and directed to take quarters in a damaged house not far from the railway station, the Rue du Saumon. This had a large cellar which connected to the cellars of adjacent houses, and one could walk for considerable distances through them. Although we explored these thoroughly, as also the rooms of the house, we found nothing of use or value. The houses had been occupied by Germans, French and British troops in turn, so had been well ransacked. Drawers and desks had been turned out and their contents strewn about the floors. All I have now are a few picture post-cards salved from the litter. Many of the papers were bills and order forms for earthenware tiles and bricks for which Arras was famous. Papers such as these were found in quite a number of the houses, which indicated how large the local industry had been.

A few years ago I again visited Arras with my daughter, Pamela. We saw this house and also the houses in Achicourt. I was surprised to see how faithfully these buildings had been restored to what must have been their original style and indeed not much if any modernisation or alterations seemed to have been carried out, the character of the old town and its suburbs having been retained.

The railway station at Arras was a shambles and the line of course out of use. There were a number of small unexploded aerial bombs lying about, being of brass with brass fins. These small bombs would at that time have been dropped over the side by hand from fighter planes.

We slept on the floor of the empty front room of the house. On most nights the station and vicinity were shelled or bombed, and my companions would take their blankets down to the cellar, but I preferred to stay in the room, probably feeling too lazy or sleepy to trouble. The battalion was now out of the line and ensconced in the Schramm Barracks. The city was crowded with troops of various units including Canadians and South Africans, but hardly any civilians had as yet returned.

We soon left for other areas, moving from place to place and eventually once more back to Arras. I find that about this period I have a very hazy memory of events, everything now being mixed up as regards places and sequence of events. I will, however, endeavour to tell of what I can still recall.

We were for a time encamped in wooden huts beside the Lens-Arras road and a few miles from the city. Our carpenters made a wooden cross, which I coated with white paint and inscribed in black lettering the rank, name and number of each of the 30 men killed at Neuville Vitasse, 9th April 1917, with RIP at the top, and underneath I added the words '*Dulce et decorum est pro patria mori*'. This was only one cross of the many I was to inscribe during the next twelve months. I also painted signboards for the various messes for the officers and sergeants, and for the cobbler, tailor, QM stores, etc. etc., a nice quiet occupation which relieved me of many other boring parades and duties whilst the battalion were out of the line at so called 'rest'.

We were soon to be moved up to the line again in different sectors from time-to-time. When relieved we spent more or less quiet periods both in Arras and in various camps, mostly in Nissen huts out in the surrounding plains, but adjacent to the Lens-Arras Road or the Cambrai Road. The front line periods were in the Wancourt and Monchy areas. An attack was made on Cavalry Farm at Monchy, but was held up by heavy machine gun fire, some of our men getting through to our objective but eventually having to retire to our original positions. It was here that one huge shell buried a whole platoon of 20 Kensingtons, who were, however, dug out unharmed except for a few bad cases of shell-shock. We lost about 90 men in this operation.

About this time we had bad news of several very grave and depressing events. First the mutiny of the French Army, exhausted and dispirited by their frightful losses and strains at Verdun, the Somme and Champaigne, and who refused to take part in any more attacks, being willing only to hold the line as it was. Then the news that the Russians were weakening and if defeated would release a million Germans to fight against our front. Then that some of the Australians had mutinied against their officers for some reason or other, and actually set fire to camps, English battalions having to be sent to quieten them down and restore order.

One of the worst pieces of news to us was that of the strike by coal miners in England. This really did shock and disgust us. We, including many of these miners' sons and relatives were sacrificing our lives and limbs and enduring unspeakable horrors and conditions to shield the British people from slavery or worse. These strikers were deliberately putting a spoke in the wheel, holding up the manufacture of weapons and ammunition to say nothing of fuel for our naval and merchant ships bringing vital supplies of arms and food across the oceans at great danger to themselves from submarine attack. When questioned about this their miserable whine was that they were acting in the interest of their sons when they returned from the War, while in fact they were doing their callous best to destroy them.

Many of us will never forget or forgive this betrayal. However badly the miners may have been paid at that time, others including their mates and sons who were doing magnificent tunnelling work in the trenches, were sacrificing themselves and everything they cherished getting a pittance of a very few shillings a week. The time to strike is not when the country is in peril.

Yet another piece of news which disgusted us was the incredible action of our Government in selling huge quantities of cement to the Dutch, knowing that this was to be passed to the Germans for the construction of their much vaunted Hindenburg Line, against which we were expected to, and did, sacrifice thousands of lives to attack and overwhelm.

You may imagine the effect on us of these unpleasant pieces of news. It seemed that we were indeed out on a limb and would have to carry on the War by ourselves. Most of us were by then already resigned to our fate, there seeming to be no likelihood of peace, the war being a deadlock, and that we would never see England again, unless on a stretcher. In spite of this I am sure that we were grimly determined to stick it out to the end, and in fact I never heard anyone even suggesting that we should do otherwise.

Under the City of Arras there were many long tunnels and caves, partly constructed as a sewage system. These tunnels were connected to many of the cellars and were in the past lit by electricity. There was also a light rail system installed therein. These tunnels led outside Arras and opened to the old British trench system. There was room to accommodate thousands of troops and on occasion sheltered our battalion.

I took the opportunity one afternoon to visit the centre of the city which at the time was crowded with thousands of men belonging to various units, mostly Canadian, with some South African, Scottish and Welsh regiments. The walls of the old theatre were still standing, with remains of theatrical bills still adorning them. An army concert party were performing inside. I entered the large enclosure, its walls tattered and open to the sky, the roof being entirely missing. The crowded audience seemed mostly Canadian. The only turn I remember was a remarkably good imitation of Charlie Chaplin; it was so very like the real thing that I still wonder if it was indeed the famous comedian himself giving the performance.

Although a few long range shells occasionally fell on the town, I was amazed that the Germans missed such a marvellous opportunity to bombard it thoroughly. This would have caused enormous casualties in so crowded an area. Perhaps there was some mysterious reason for not so doing.

During one period of rest in the Schramm Barracks we had experience of the new long range shells now being used by the Germans. Several of these fell in the vicinity and we were intrigued at hearing the shell bursts before the sound of their approach, due to the velocity of the missile being faster than the speed of sound. A few of these would arrive each evening, one exploding in the kitchens just across the yard opposite our building. Fortunately there were no casualties, although some of the ovens and cookers were ruined.

About this time I heard that my young cousin Johnny Reeve was now in Rouen, he having joined a cyclist battalion. I was glad that he had now come out to join Frankie Jones and myself, but hoped that he would not eventually be sent to the battle area.

I have not told about our own Divisional concert party, called 'Bow Bells' and made up of a professional entertainer named Harry Brandon and three others, two being female impersonators (one being appropriately from the London Scottish) and very like the real thing, in fact similar to and a forerunner of Danny La Rue. His favourite tune was:

> Do you remember, when I first came to town, take a look at me now.
> Do you remember, my first simple gown, take a look ... etc. etc.

They gave us quite a few enjoyable evenings, whenever opportunity occurred, in various camps – sometimes in a hut or large marquee and sometimes from the top of a GS waggon. Their official duty was that of Divisional laundry and they were employed in fumigating our blankets – a very useful and effective job. I am afraid their rare efforts on our socks and shirts were not so successful – the shrinkage of these articles being disastrous.

At one of the camps near a village behind Arras we had some rather embarrassing visitors. Our latrine was the usual deep trench surmounted by a pole supported by trestles, the area being screened by canvas. Two or three young women would arrive from the village and walk along the seated occupants selling chocolate from the trays hung from their shoulders. This they did quite unconcernedly joining in with the inevitable banter. What intrigued us most was that they then visited the officers' quarters, spending about an hour in the huts before leaving with their empty trays. There was of course much speculation on our part as to what transpired during these periods.

While on the subject I must mention the occasion when one of the small men drafted to us from the Bantam Regiment and whose boots were at the cobblers, borrowed those of a comrade. Visiting the muddy latrine and perching himself on the pole, his short legs preventing his feet from resting on the ground, he lost balance and fell backwards into the disgusting contents of the pit. He had to be helped out, leaving his companion's boots, which were several sizes too large for him, in the bottom of the morass. What occurred afterwards between him and his pal I never learned, but expect the air was pretty thick and no doubt his ear also! Incidents such as this, although often rather crude, gave us much amusement and helped to relieve the otherwise dreadful monotony and discomfort of our lives.

There was a rumour going that the Germans were leaving booby traps as they retreated and we were warned to be on our guard against this. The rumour turned out to be a fact. Once when occupying the ruins of a large farm just taken from the enemy we found that an open well in the farmyard had been poisoned and a human carcase had been thrown into the well. Our medical section tested the water and condemned it. Also in an outhouse of the farm, which had been the sleeping quarters of some German troops, was a small home-made oil lamp, which when lit by one of our men, exploded, turning his face, hands and uniform a bright yellow, but otherwise not harming him. Also in an abandoned German trench abutting the Arras - Cambrai road was a trip wire stretching at knee height across the trench bottom, attached to a cluster of several stick-bombs half concealed at a dug-out entrance. There was no one in authority available to report to at the time, and I left well alone, the matter soon escaping my memory, there being plenty to occupy my attention in other directions. Anyway, it was pretty obvious in the daylight. In other instances grenades had been discovered attached to doors and other objects likely to be moved by the unwary. It paid to be suspicious of anything lying around.

Artillery were dotted about over the desertlike plains and low valleys, and we would sometimes experience the thrilling sight of teams of artillery horses galloping at top speed, taking field guns to their positions or withdrawing them. The speed and efficiency of these operations was amazing, the guns being limbered up and rushed away in the matter of a minute or so, the gunners seated on the limbers and gun carriages. This was reminiscent of the displays at the miliary Tournament in peace time, and also of the pictures by War artists of old time battles.

We would sometimes hear of atrocities, but I never had first hand experience of any. For instance, we were told of the Australian soldier who was captured and crucified on a barn door. The

Australians, incensed by this episode took a terrible revenge on a company of Germans trapped against barbed wire entanglements and who tried to surrender. The Aussies set up their machine guns and mercilessly annihilated them. Another time a German raiding party was captured by a Scottish regiment, who made the unfortunate men return towards their own lines and shot them down as they tried to get through the barbed wire. There were of course the tales of German brutality told by some of the French villagers, but we did not know how much of this was fact or fiction. In those days there was often a great deal of chivalry shown by both sides, particularly in regard to captured airmen.

The telling of the narrative may seem rather erratic and disjointed, but so indeed was our own experience with its frequent and short moves to different sectors of the line, periods of rest in various camps and villages, days and nights of acute discomfort in and about the line; often in heavy rain, mud and water without cover, meagre rations and foul drinking water, to say nothing of the danger and noise of bombardments. Death and wounds, some hideous, were commonplace. Illness such as trench fever, trench feet and common ailments had to be endured, and even the worst cases could have no attention until we were back in a rest area. Then unless a man was really seriously ill, the only remedy seemed to be the well-known 'number-nine' pill, prescribed as a 'Cure-all'.

Gas shelling was now becoming increasingly intense causing many casualties. One could detect gas not only from the curious 'plop' of the explosion, but also from the strong smell which persisted long after the shell had fallen. Peculiarly this smell did not seem the same to different persons. To me it was rather like tangerines, to others like onions, or mustard and so on. The gas in concentration would affect the eyes, often causing temporary blindness, the nose, throat and lungs, also any part of the body damp from perspiration, causing much soreness with red and inflamed patches. We often had to don our gas-masks, these somewhat clouding the vision and slowing down progress owing to the difficulty of breathing by mouth through the tube.

The entrances to dug-outs and shelters would, when occasion permitted, be draped with blankets saturated in a smelly chemical and would be sprayed occasionally by men deputised as gas orderlies. There would be an empty brass shell-case hung outside, which when beaten would act as a gong to give warning of gas. At some of the reserve camps a few miles behind the line these precautions were also taken, as gas-shelling was by no means confined only to the trenches.

It was quite usual to hear and even to look back and see huge explosions as the enemy guns found the immense dumps of shells stored behind the lines. Some of these dumps must have covered an acre or two of ground, stacked high, and often with dividing earth walls. It was disheartening to see the destruction in the space of a few seconds of enormous masses of ammunition and to think of the great labour and care that must have gone into its manufacture and transport across the sea from Britain and America. This destruction was not of course confined only to our own dumps, we could observe the same thing happening on the German side, a much more cheerful event for us.

There was one such explosion on the Cambrai-Arras roadside, just on the outskirts of the town, many of the shells, including the huge 'flying pigs' lying scattered about unexploded; the 'flying pig' was a great fat sausage shaped mortar bomb, our own equivalent of the *minnenwerfer*.

In the forward area many of the recently abandoned trenches were used for access purposes and for sheltering the support and reserve troops. These became thick with mud, covering all kinds of debris, often whole boxes of ammunition, cartridges, hand-grenades and so on. Often there was a soft, rubbery feeling under foot similar to standing on an inflated mattress; this would indicate a dead body in the bottom of the trench, having been trampled deeper in the mud by the feet of perhaps hundreds of men passing over it. Sometimes an arm or a leg would be protruding. No one had time or inclination to do anything about this. It soon became a common experience and accepted with indifference.

On taking over an enemy trench one of the first tasks was to dig or cut fire steps into the side now facing the Germans, as of course the original fire step was on the wrong side for us, and the parados would have to be converted into a parapet with the earth thrown out, making use of the empty sandbags carried by the assaulting troops. The heart-shaped spades, called grafting tools, would here come into use, together with our entrenching tools which were part of our normal equipment. We all had extra burdens of one sort or another to carry into action. There were hand grenades, spades, extra ammunition, sometimes short scaling ladders, rockets, stokes gun shells, Lewis Guns with tripods and extra pans of ammunition; all this in addition to our own equipment including haversack, ground sheet, water bottle, entrenching tool, gas mask, cartridge pouches, rifle, bayonet and steel helmet, to say nothing of pounds of clay around our heavy boots and on our clothing.

In a day or so, often before, the momentum of the advance would slow down, the enemy falling back to well prepared positions and usually counter attacking, sometimes retaking part of the ground. Dangerous salients and gaps between units would occur and many minor engagements would take place to try and eliminate these salients and so straighten the line.

Some of the prisoners appeared to be very young, almost boys, and also there were older, bearded men, some looking well past their prime. The Germans must have been feeling the effects of these fierce battles combined with their very heavy losses on the Russian front. Their best regiments, as I have said, were composed of fine physical specimens, tough and stubborn fighters, their non-commissioned officers seeming very proud and arrogant, strictly trained and disciplined. Many of the dead and also prisoners had the black-and-white ribbon of the iron cross showing at a button-hole. These seem to have been handed out fairly liberally. I was sometimes tempted to take one as a souvenir, but could not at that time bring myself to despoil a brave man of his honours. I could not help having respect for the slain. After all most of them were, and looked, harmless little citizens until dragged willy-nilly into this senseless holocaust. I would look down at the body of a young man; just a useless carcase. Someone at home would not yet know they were never to see him again. Parents, perhaps a wife and children, would grieve deeply over him. Only a short time ago this dead thing would have been talking, laughing and joking with his companions, or writing a letter home. Now it was suddenly and hideously finished, not by accident but by design. And for what? We began to curse all politicians and rulers, feeling that if we could get them out here to see at first hand the horrible results of greed, ignorance, incompetence and ambition, they would try and stop the slaughter at once. In the meantime we would have to carry on to the end in the 'War to end War'. How farcical!

Although it is doubtful if there were many unbelievers on the battlefield, there must have been moments of doubt. I often wondered how the Almighty could condone such suffering and distress, particularly on so vast a scale. Many a mortally wounded man lying in agony for hours or even days and nights unattended in no-man's-land must have cried 'Oh God, why hast thou abandoned me'. These men also bore their cross!

One night I had the almost unique experience of getting a grand-stand view of a duel between two opposing front-line trenches. Four of us had been detailed to take stone jars of rum up to the support line, extending across both sides of a long straight road, if I remember rightly the Arras-Cambrai road. It was a dark night, the road showing faintly before us, the country being flat and bare on each side. We reached a point where the road sloped slightly downwards, being elevated a few feet above the surrounding countryside. We were not sure of the point to which we had been directed, but should have been met there by one of the men. We passed this point, not noticing the trench in the dark and came to a trestle of barbed wire right across the road. Some distance beyond this barrier we stopped for a moment wondering if we were walking into the German lines. Everything was uncannily silent, the faint white of the road stretching straight ahead. Suddenly a terrific din and flashes of light occurred on both sides of the road, immediately answered by a similar outburst along a parallel line about 50 yards or so ahead. Bright lights and sparks were arching up from both lines as all manner of missiles were being fired off and landing with loud explosions. The firing seemed to commence from about 20 yards away on each side of the road, nothing landing on or near the road itself, where we were standing looking down into the British trench on each side, all brightly lit up. It was exactly like an immense firework display, and we could see the men busily at work with their trench mortars and rifle grenades. Peculiarly I felt perfectly safe, like a spectator at a firework show.

I was so intrigued with the scene that I felt no anxiety about my own safety. I cannot understand why we were not perceived and mown down. Perhaps the Jerries had indeed seen us but were not sure to which side we belonged. The absence of shell fire must have been due to the close proximity of the opposing trenches, the artillery not firing for fear of shelling their own men, or for the fact that the sudden outburst had not given them time to get into action. However, we soon came to our senses and made our way back to the barbed wire barrier, when the engagement stopped almost as suddenly as it had started and all was again silent. A short way past the barrier we were challenged by the man who should have intercepted us before, and we left our jars of rum to his keeping and set off to join our section.

Almost daily during fine weather we would be entertained by one or more duels between a couple of airmen, sometimes so low that we could hear their machine guns firing. Large groups of shrapnel would bespatter the blue sky with their tiny white clouds of smoke. Occasionally one of the planes would be brought down either by shrapnel or the opponent. These airmen would incite our admiration – they would fight to a finish or until one would run out of ammunition and turn off for home with its opponent on its tail. On more than one occasion we would see one airman deliberately fly into the other, both coming down together. The German Fokker planes at that time had a great advantage, being able to fire directly to the front through their propellers which were synchronised with their machine guns, then an innovation.

We would sometimes be camped next to the London Scottish. I would like to say that I find much of the pipers' music very stirring, but we were sometimes treated for hours to most tuneless and monotonous dirges which I can only think were practice exercises. Several times I ran into an old school friend, Alec Campbell. He told me of a recent daylight raid in which the Scottish took over cans of petrol which they pitched down the dug-out entrances, followed by hand grenades. I met Campbell on the railway station at Ruislip one day long after the war.

At a village near Arras I ran into another young school acquaintance named Pearce. His brother, a cocky and aggressive boy, had forced a fight on me, egged on by his hero worshipping parents, who quickly called him off when they saw he was getting the worst of the encounter. A most uncalled for attack. Why it was I do not know, but most of my scraps were begun by young braggarts and bullies, but I always seemed well able to hold my own, especially later on after I had gained experience in friendly (although sometimes rather rough) boxing bouts with my companions. I must have appeared simple in those days, and never quarrelled unless provoked. One young bully said in surprise, 'I didn't know you could fight.' Neither did I at the time.

In France there was a big young fellow who had recently been detailed to our Regimental police. He was very arrogant and was soon dominating the others and evidently not popular with them. One day he stood at the entrance to our shack, making sarcastic and derogatory remarks. I was sitting on the ground writing a letter home, and feeling very irritated with his behaviour, I got up and told him to buzz off, striking him heavily with my shoulder. He went backwards, catching his foot on a piece of wood by the door, falling full length on his back. I squared up expecting him to get up and attack me, but to my surprise he refused to fight and tried to make friends with me. My companions afterwards warned me to be careful as this fellow was a stoker in civilian life. The next day one of the police told me he had heard what had happened and was very glad I had dealt with the chap and that it was time someone put him in his place.

If I remember rightly, it was along the Arras-Cambrai road towards Monchy that we came across a small defile or valley leading off the main road. It was not much more than a sunken track, surprisingly green with grass and entered through a field gate. It led perhaps a couple of hundred yards before turning right to the plain beyond. The whole length of this track was littered with dead cavalry horses, swords and rifles. Obviously a troop of cavalry had been ambushed from the far end by machine guns and annihilated. This was another instance of the futility of using cavalry in modern trench warfare. Unfortunately Sir Douglas Haig, being a cavalryman himself, was obsessed with the dream of a cavalry breakthrough, which of course was never to be fully realised. Horses were far too conspicuous and vulnerable to machine gun and artillery fire, although they did once have some measure of success during the attack later on at Cambrai. Many of the horse regiments were dismounted and used as infantry.

Troops coming out of action for a short spell in reserve had to be content with living in the open, sometimes in the remains of old battered trenches and shell-holes, often under long range shell-fire. In wet muddy weather this can be a miserable hell. Often the so-called 'rest' would only be for a few hours, or a night or two, orders coming for a return to the front line, either to the same or a nearby sector, until at last relieved for a spell in the back areas, sometimes in an evacuated village, or if lucky where there were a few civilians and an estaminet or two.

I would sometimes think of my parents at home and be glad to believe that they were snug and warm, and wonder if they ever imagined what we were enduring over here. The plaintive wail of our fat little Bantam exclaiming 'If only my muvver could see me now' seemed very appropriate and afforded some comic relief, in spite of the pathos.

Of course things were a good deal better in the dry weather. It is remarkable how we escaped crippling rheumatism and even the common cold, which was a rare complaint. This must have been due to the hard living, fresh air and simple food, toughening up the constitution.

One instance comes to mind, but I cannot recall exactly when or where. We had experienced a very trying time in and about the line during wet weather. We dragged back some miles, soaked and heavy with mud, arriving totally exhausted at a derelict farm. The barns and sheds were quite extensive, the road through the farm resembling a small village. My company were billeted in the loft of a huge barn, with a scattering of dirty straw on the floor. We had arrived at dusk and soon had our pieces of candle alight. I always marvelled that these barns did not catch fire from the candles and cigarettes among the straw and woodwork. The field kitchens had arrived from the transport lines and we queued up for a pint of hot cocoa and some bread and cheese. It was the first hot drink we had received for a week or more. As soon as we got back to our billets another call came to fetch our mess-tin lids, and we were served with a welcome large tot of rum.

After a good night's sleep, bacon and tea for breakfast, we fell in to resume our march to the rear areas and a somewhat more civilised existence for a while. This gave us a chance to clean up and feel more like living human beings once more. Until next time! This was typical of life during the big battles and much different from the more orderly existence when serving on quiet sectors where things were more or less static, with a regular routine of four days each in front line, support line and reserve in a small village or camp.

One day the pioneer sergeant, whom we rarely saw, arrived and led us to an apparently deserted locality which had been recently evacuated by the enemy. The country was flat and featureless except for a couple of ruined houses, one on each side of an open road. We settled down in one of these houses and Harry Kay and I were told to commence digging a tunnel from the cellar to stretch under the road and connect up to the other house. Armed with pick and grafting spades we started work, and it was soon apparent that Harry was conversant with tunnel work. He worked on the face and I cleared the rubble. After a few feet the tunnel roofing began crumbling and falling in. The chaps upstairs were busy cutting lengths of 4″ x 2″ quartering which had been dumped at the site, Harry expertly inserted these wooden props into the sides and roof of the tunnel, but as the falls were getting dangerous he would not let me into the short length of tunnel now formed, and insisted on working inside by himself. One heavy fall partially buried him and after I had helped him out the sergeant came along to cancel the work.

I believe the idea had been to use the buildings as a battalion or brigade headquarters but the position was too obvious in the middle of such featureless land, besides which our activities had no doubt been observed, as we had received the attention of several salvos of shells from the enemy artillery and were glad when after a few days the operation was called off. I am telling this as it was one of several instances where Harry would take on dangerous jobs by himself. In spite of his often unscrupulous behaviour towards outsiders and their belongings, he was loyal to his pals and a really rough diamond.

We stayed on the Arras front until the beginning of June. I remember the time when we were relieved. Our section was occupying a flimsy corrugated iron shelter in the side of a shallow ditch or half-dug trench on the ridge at Beaurains. That late afternoon a section from the relieving battalion arrived to take over. The enemy must have seen the activity, as they started shelling the vicinity. We stopped about a hundred yards away while one of our chaps went back to retrieve, I think, his cigarettes. After a few minutes he returned and said the shelter had received a direct hit which killed the new occupants. That was a lucky escape for us and we had got out just in time.

We spent the next week or so in various quiet villages behind Arras – a restful change in green surroundings, but then returned to the Beaurains area in reserve, a camp now having been erected near this village on the site of the old battlefield. The weather had turned appalling and everywhere was flooded. Trenches in the front line were confused, enemy positions not properly known, our trenches in places being very exposed to observation, but thanks to the weather things were fairly quiet. It was however utterly miserable in the heavy rain and we were completely soaked and covered with mud from head to foot.

We were now in the Wancourt area. There was great difficulty in getting food and water up to the line. Although this period was comparatively quiet, we did sustain a number of casualties, mostly from machine gun fire when getting across exposed gaps between uncompleted or broken down sections of trench. I remember one very exposed place on which a machine gun had been trained, probably with fixed sights. We had to carry supplies over this at night, and would throw them over the gap and run across as quickly as possible. There was a strong smell of rum here, several of the jars being broken from this rough treatment. The battalion was relieved at the beginning of July and we were utterly worn out during the drag back via Neuville Vitasse and Beaurains, the road and tracks being quagmires. Many of the fellows were suffering from trench feet. We thankfully sank down to rest at the new camp at Beaurains. Many of the chaps had such bad feet that they were forced to use their rifles as props to help themselves along.

As everyone was dead-beat we were allowed the whole night and next day to rest and get as dry as possible. Then for two days we worked hard at getting ourselves cleaned up. The first day was spent in getting the thick coating of mud off our clothing, boots and equipment with the aid of our jack-knives. The following day we were expected to complete cleaning clothing and equipment, have weapons thoroughly cleaned and oiled, buttons and buckles brightly polished ready for evening inspection, after which some genius issued lumps of khaki 'blanco' to mix into a paste and apply to our webbing equipment. All this kept us very busy, but the resulting smart appearance no doubt helped to boost our morale. We then literally hobbled painfully through Arras and either embussed or entrained (I forget which) to Liencourt. We passed an anti-aircraft gun outside Arras, which was firing at a German plane overhead. The shells were bursting very near the plane which came immediately over the gun and suddenly dived straight down to within about twenty feet of it, scattering the crew in all directions, when to our amazement it suddenly darted off and away. A very daring piece of airmanship in those days and probably the only way to stop the gun from firing.

VI

Will It Never End?

From Liencourt we entrained to St Omer, thence marching to the villages of Houle and Moule for training and a restful period of a few days in the beautiful July sunshine amidst lovely green meadows and river, where some of us bathed and fished. I had a line, float and hook in my pocket book, and cutting a branch for rod, fished with another enthusiast, but caught nothing, although we could see shoals of very large bream in the clear water close to the bank. Some of the fellows were more successful, using hand grenades to stun the fish – a very unsportsmanlike method, besides being a waste of good ammunition. One chap made a very fine watercolour sketch of a picturesque stone bridge over a stream.

We left Moule and embussed for Abeele and thence towards the third battle of Ypres. Our vehicles were old London buses painted grey. I had a seat on top of an open double-decker. It would have been like a holiday outing if it had not been for the knowledge of our destination. We passed along good country roads, past delightful green meadows and woods. There were many low telephone wires crossing the roads and we had to keep a very sharp eye open and prepare to crouch in our seats to avoid being decapitated.

I remember reaching the village of Abeele and crossing a stone bridge over a river, a sentry box at each end of the bridge. This was the Franco-Belgian border and we were in Belgium for the first time. From here we marched to Steenvoorde. The Belgian inhabitants did not seem to welcome us and looked very surly, perhaps not to be wondered at as Flanders has been the battleground of Europe over the centuries. We were told that many of them were suspected of being spies. The inmates of an estaminet told us when and where we were going and seemed to know a good deal more of our business than we ourselves did. The peasants would stand at their cottage doors scowling at us as we marched past.

Arriving at Mic-Mac Camp near Dickebusch we stayed for about three days in Nissen huts. The surrounding fields were flat, bleak and muddy with many water-filled ditches. The huts were fitted with double tiers of wire bunks. The top bunks were the best as the whole place was alive with fat lice and these would fall like raindrops onto the unfortunates occupying the lower bunks. At night we were visited by one or two enemy aircraft with bombs. The village of Ouderdom was a mile or two away, over which a huge shrapnel shell would occasionally burst high in the sky, leaving behind a large black smoke cloud. We were marched in platoons to this village and sent into a big disused brewery, getting a bath in wooden tubs filled with hot water, with plenty of soap – a rare treat. A clean set of underclothes and socks (much shrunken) were issued and we felt wonderfully clean once more. However, we returned to our huts, which had been thoroughly drenched in our absence with what I was told to be D.D.T., immediately feeling plops falling onto our caps – the lice had found us again and we were soon infested even more so than before.

Journalists and writers of popular songs fostered a rather false, if romantic idea among civilians, of our soldiers marching into battle with cheerful songs and jokes. While this was true up to a point, it certainly was not the case when troops were approaching the actual battle zones where attacks were imminent or in progress. As one got nearer the line, with its ominous sights and sounds, the atmosphere became one of grim reality and men's thoughts tended to turn inwards. This was most marked on many individuals, the strain and anxiety showing in their faces and by their quiet and thoughtful demeanour. This attitude was quite common just prior to taking part in an assault.

No doubt the first-time experience was the worst with the thought of going into the unknown, of unseen dangers and horrors yet to be faced. I have recounted my own sudden feeling of fear on that one night when the full significance of what lay ahead struck me with such sudden force, but which had vanished by next morning, never to return with such intensity. This feeling was replaced by the gnawing anxiety which every virgin soldier must experience before his first encounter; that is, how he will react to the occasion – would he be able to face up to the dangers or would he show cowardice? This particular anxiety does not recur after his first battle, for he has by then found the answer.

After withdrawal from the battle area, if there had been heavy casualties many of the fellows would again be quiet and withdrawn, thinking of their awful experiences and of the companions lost. This was particularly noticeable among the older and more sober-minded men, some of whom had wives and children to worry about. Most of the younger men and the hardened veterans quickly recovered their spirits and morale.

On the third day we girded up and commenced our march to Ypres, passing Brigadier General Lewis, a former Kensington, now with another brigade. It was 15th August and the weather looked very dull and threatening. We approached Ypres through the flat countryside until we reached a junction with what was apparently a main road, and turning left proceeded in open formation with a good interval between platoons. We were told that we were about to pass Shrapnel Corner. On the left was the long high wall of the rampart surrounding the city. I am not sure now whether it was brick or stone, but brick I believe. The right-hand side of the road, alongside a moat, ran parallel to the battle front. It was bordered by the stumps of smashed trees, beyond which and across the moat were large pools and muddy shell-torn earth with here and there duck-board tracks leading off to the battle area. The roadside was littered with dozen of overturned and smashed up vehicles and guns, the teams of horribly mutilated horses with huge gaping wounds, often completely disemboweled.

These sights should have filled me with terror, but actually I felt quite calm and fascinated at being in the famous battlefield of Ypres where British and French had struggled with Germans, backwards and forwards for three years; never letting the Germans gain control of the City, but being unable to drive them back for more than a few miles. This had entailed terrible losses on both sides, but Ypres was a key point to be defended against any attempt by the enemy to attack the Channel ports.

We reached a large gateway in the rampart which I think must have been the Menin Gate. We did not enter this, and indeed never did enter the City itself. We turned right, across a crude wooden bridge over the moat and on to a duck-board track crossing flat marshy ground, and a few yards to the left of the large Zillebeke Lake. Someone said we were near Hellfire Corner. As we proceeded in single file, several shells fell close by.

Our party were led by a young lieutenant, the RSM being with us. The officer ducked every time a shell burst near us, and the sergeant major shouted angrily at him each time he did this and told him to keep his head up. The poor fellow must have felt very scared and also humiliated, but I must say I felt rather contemptuous of him for showing his fear in front of the men he was supposed to be leading. Fortunately most of our other officers were brave and disciplined men, many of them exceptionally so.

Ahead of us the ground rose and we arrived on top of a mound or hill, entering a deep trench system which appeared to be some kind of redoubt. It had now become dark and a furious bombardment commenced, fortunately falling just short of our trenches. Huge flashes of yellow and reddish explosions just below the edge, the ground sloping fairly steeply downwards. These glimpses were enough and I settled down with the other chaps on the bottom of the six foot trench. The shelling ceased after a while, and during the night a tank crawled onto the ground above, stopping just a few feet from the parados, looming just above me as a dark silhouette. I felt a bit uncomfortable about this, and hoped the driver was able to well control the steering of this cumbersome machine. I must have slept very heavily that night, as by morning I found that the tank had gone. These tanks made a terrible noise when in motion, and could be heard miles away, so I must have slept very soundly indeed.

The weather was still dull and the surrounding country very bare, the ground having been pulverised, and churned up, full of shell-holes and craters, waterlogged, with a few duckboard tracks, running towards the Westhoek Ridge ahead. Batteries of artillery guns were firing from their positions in the open with no attempt at camouflage. Someone said that our overnight position was known as Half-way House. I am not sure even today – it might have been Stirling Castle. Our battalion headquarters staff were in the entrance to a sort of cave or tunnel, which was said to lead into Ypres itself, although I doubt this as the terrain below was so waterlogged.

The companies started moving off towards Westhoek Ridge, when someone brought the news that a shell had fallen just round the bend of our trench and that our commanding officer Major Flower had been killed, the Battalion Major and the Adjutant, together with Regimental Sergeant Major Blake wounded, leaving us therefore with no senior officers. Command was taken over by Captain Venables temporarily until Captain Shaw was sent from Brigade to take over. Heavy fire was taking place on the Westhoek Ridge and we understood that an attack was in progress by two other brigades.

The Germans were shelling the whole area in front of us, as we started off down the slope to the low ground below, making use of a single duck-board track before it disappeared and we had to make our way through the mud and shell holes. We went in small parties of four or five men and were told to keep 30 yard intervals between each squad. I had charge of three other men and the corporal followed with four men. The ground was in a shocking state, but we emerged into the Ypres-Menin Road which led straight on to and over the ridge. This road had been constructed very solidly and was raised several feet above the surrounding marshy land, the road being comparatively dry underfoot and withstanding shell-fire much better than the softer surroundings.

There was a wide view on either side. Batteries of field guns, fully exposed without any cover or camouflage were firing, sinking deeper into the mud at each discharge. The craters and shell-holes were full of water, the remains of shattered guns, debris and dead bodies, both British and German, lying about, some half submerged in water. Many of the wounded and even unhurt men were drowned in these mud and water filled holes, being unable to pull themselves out, loaded as they were with equipment and weapons. Teams of horses were somehow managing to get guns into the morass, heaven knows how.

Over on our left was what remained of Hooge, and just off the roadside a ruined building (which incidentally someone also called Half-Way House) now being used as a dressing station. In front of this were dozens of wounded men lying on stretchers, awaiting to be taken further back to the ambulances. Some were completely covered in blankets and so would be dead. Many Germans were among the wounded. Numbers of walking wounded were arriving and waiting about to have their wounds attended to.

We proceeded up the road keeping the required 30 yards behind the squad in front, which was led by one of our oldest soldiers, Sergeant Bryant of the regimental police. Shells were falling all over the area, some on the road and verges. Here and there a tree stump was standing alongside the road, not many more than a foot or so high. Hundreds of shells were falling into the pools and holes, many of them failing to explode, but sending up high geysers of water into the air. Lines of German prisoners were filing down from the ridge ahead, passing us without a glance and all apparently immune to their own shell-fire. They were no doubt mostly in a state of shock and glad to be going towards safety.

The strain of the barrage was so great that I tried to shut my mind from all that was going on around, making it as blank as possible and looking only at the ground immediately in front of me. Every now and again the squad ahead would stop, and we would get into the nearest shell hole waiting for them to get going again. Fortunately most of the shell holes along the road were fairly dry. Only a few khaki-clad men passed us, and these were all walking wounded. We did not stop to assist any casualties, as this was not allowed when going up to the line, and this task had to be left to whatever stretcher bearers might come along.

As we got nearer the top of the ridge, we passed several abandoned German concrete pill boxes, and we looked into some of these; they nearly all contained the bodies of one or two British dead, some obviously abandoned there on stretchers. There were dead men of many different units, showing that assault after assault must have been made in attempting to capture this Westhoek Ridge. As we got near the top we saw the remains of Inverness Copse abutting the road on the left, and what appeared to be the battered parapet of a trench on each side of the road and along the length of the Ridge.

Sergeant Bryant's squad stopped just short of the wood and he waved to me to come on, but obeying instructions I refused to move until he had gone forward. The ridge was still being heavily shelled and as we approached the top, machine gun fire was zipping past our heads. Someone told us to enter the trench on the right, where we found a very large concrete pill-box, still intact, the narrow horizontal firing embrasures facing towards the British side, and blind to the rear (German front), which was just as well. There were several other Kensingtons in this pill-box, but the body of a man from some county regiment lay on a stretcher on top of a concrete shelf, where it remained for some hours before stretcher bearers arrived and took it away. We settled down on the floor, and I noticed several fat maggots crawling about. I picked up a German field postcard for a souvenir which I still have. It was very similar to our own, with the stilted sentences to be ticked or crossed out.

A fellow came in and told us that Sergeant Bryant had just been killed – he was the second sergeant the police had lost. It seemed that it was just as well I had not taken my squad forward to join his as he had signalled. The shelling was so near and heavy that none of us ventured outside. At least two direct hits were received with terrific impact, one in front and one on top. I was never so grateful to the Germans for providing such a strong piece of concrete work. I read some time ago that the British had tried to destroy this particular pill box which dominated the Ypres-Menin road from the corner of Inverness Copse, but that it had withstood the high explosive 18 pounder shells, which were not large enough to do the job. If it had been destroyed it is unlikely that I would have survived to tell the tale. The shelling stopped towards late afternoon, and we ventured out and looked down the slope on the other side of the ridge, another almost featureless morass with a low ridge in the distance and on the right was, so we were told, the famous Hill 60, the remains of Glencorse Wood, Chateau Wood and Tower Hamlets. We must have slept soundly during the night, although I have now no recollection of this, or of receiving any rations.

We were told that in the morning an attack was to be made by another brigade in front of our position, and that if successful we were to follow this up. Our barrage opened up at dawn, and surprisingly the enemy retaliation did not reach our position on the ridge except for an occasional shell and a few bursts of machine gun fire. We had a grand-stand view of the proceedings, the heavy barrage being along a line probably about five hundred yards away on the plain below. We could see very little of what was happening on the ground, owing to the smoke of the shell fire.

An aeroplane was flying backwards and forwards along the line of the barrage, very low and actually amongst the bursting shrapnel shells. He would be spotting and reporting the progress of the action. We were admiring the bravery and daring of this pilot, when suddenly one of the wings of the plane was blown off and he plummeted to the earth in the midst of the attack. All we could see of the action were small groups of men in khaki moving about, apparently with no co-ordination, going in various directions and suddenly disappearing into the ground, then again emerging and going into another direction, to disappear once more. All very puzzling. We heard that the attack was unsuccessful, mainly due to the shocking state of the muddy ground which made movement almost impossible.

The weather now took a hand and started to drizzle, turning to steady rain, and we were told that further operations would have to be called off. Also to our relief that our brigade was to be withdrawn from the line. This was just as well, as we learned that the other battalions in our brigade had also lost some of their senior officers and were in no condition to take part in an assault without adequate leadership and control.

At dusk a runner arrived and told us to go back by the road to Ypres in independent sections. We found our corporal and his party and set off thankfully down the Menin Road, being given a farewell spray from a Jerry machine gun as we left the ridge. It was by now pouring with rain and we hoped that this would indeed prevent any further likelihood of continuing the battle for the time being, as the passage over the already marshy ground would be made impossible.

It was now dark and as we neared Half-Way House dressing station, salvos of shells fell on and beside the road ahead of us. We hesitated to decide whether to make a dash through this barrage, walk, or stay-put for a while. If we made a dash for it we might very likely run into a shell-burst, so we decided to walk through normally. We passed the ruined building which had been used as a dressing station. It had received another hit and the iron chimney-stack poking out of the roof was leaning over, but still smoking. The place was now deserted, no wounded or stretchers about. We should have turned left here on to the duck-board track by which we had previously approached, but this was now under heavy shellfire, although there was no one about.

The road ahead appeared to be fairly quiet, so we went straight ahead to Ypres, emerging at the road junction opposite the Menin Gate. Here we turned left along the city wall and proceeded to Shrapnel Corner and turned right along the road to Dickebusch, but coming across our transport lines in a field beside a ruined farm, decided to stop here and try to shelter from the drenching rain.

However, every inch of cover in and under the limbers and lorries was packed with men. We were absolutely soaked through but rather than settle down on the sodden ground I spent the rest of the night walking about, tired out and miserable.

At dawn we continued on to the camp near Dickebusch, passing a staff car complete with red-tabbed general on his way towards the City. We were indeed thankful to settle down once more, this time in a tent, where we stayed for the next day or so. We heard that we were to be withdrawn from the area, the Third Battle of Ypres having to be abandoned for the time being owing to the change in weather conditions.

Although we had taken no active part in the fighting, our losses were over 100, including all our senior officers and RSM. Once again we had one whole platoon destroyed by a single large shell. Next night the area was again visited by enemy planes and a bomb was dropped on a nearby ammunition dump, which exploded with a terrific roar, waking and shaking us all. In the morning we strolled over to the adjacent field and found that where the dump had been was now a large crater in the ground.

The loss of our commanding officer, Major Flower (an old Kensington) and of Sergeant 'Daddy' Bryant as he was affectionately called, was particularly felt by us. I was also very sorry that RSM Blake was no longer with us, as in spite of his bullying manner, common to all sergeant majors, I must admire him as a disciplinarian and a truly professional soldier. In fact my own encounters with him were never unpleasant, rather the contrary, although he would insist that my name was Sully, a fellow who was rather similar to me in appearance, but had departed from the scene a year or two before.

He always seemed to have a generous supply of rum, to which he appeared very partial, and on several occasions when I had to report to him he poured me out a liberal portion. He was very strict with the junior officers and I remember the occasion when a lieutenant loaded a personal box on to the GS waggon in defiance of regulations, and the sergeant major ordered a man to smash the box up with his foot, much to the chagrin of the unfortunate subaltern, who had to bear the embarrassment in silence. He seemed to bear a grudge against young officers, but he certainly kept them on their toes, especially on parade, when he would at times give them a severe dressing down in his loudest voice and in front of the men.

We were pleased to say good-bye to this awful sector and entrained for Watten, near St Omer, where I had previously spent such a pleasant week, and thence to Houle and by train to Bapaume, the latter journey taking over 12 hours so slow the train.

Bapaume was on the old Somme battle-field, the country still bare and devastated. The enemy had now withdrawn to high ground some miles beyond this. We were encamped near Le Transloy with the ruins of its well remembered sugar refinery. Here we made the wooden cross complete with rail for Major Dickens who had been killed the previous year on which I painted the inscription in Old English lettering. A photograph of the cross was taken, but unfortunately I did not receive a print. I wrote recently to his niece, Miss Monica Dickens, and her sister Mrs Danby supplied me with the photograph reproduced in this book.

Several of us borrowed bicycles from the signallers and took the cross several miles away to his grave which we found marked on the ridge near Leuze Wood. A number of other bodies were buried nearby, but were now unable to be identified. While there we took the opportunity to explore the vicinity once more. Long grass and weeds now covered the ground and some of the tree stumps in the woods had even sprouted green leaves. Much of the debris had evidently been cleared away and bodies disposed of. Rats had returned and had dug holes into the unmarked graves scattered about. We did find one skeleton, that of a German lying face downwards, still with his steel helmet and only a few metal buttons lying under the bones. The uniform and other clothing had completely disintegrated. This body had evidently been overlooked by the clearing parties, probably Chinese labourers.

We visited the ruins of Les Boeufs, the small church only a mound of rubble, and someone had placed its bell on top of the mound. Nearby were the remains of a small roundabout, still standing by the roadside. A short distance away was a battered trench with a British tank still lying across where it had broken down trying to get out of the trench. A few yards away was a smashed shelter – we moved a corrugated iron sheet and found it covered with a mass of large blue-bottles. A few Mills hand grenades were lying about. I pulled the pin of one and threw it, but it failed to explode – the lever and spring had no doubt rusted up. I hope that no French farmer eventually hit this with his plough. At Aeroplane Trench the plane was still standing, looking quite serviceable. German dug-outs looked tempting to explore, but were probably by now in danger of collapse. Our corporal made one or two tentative efforts to descend a dug-out, but found the air too foul, so we left these well alone. We passed Combles with the ruins of its sugar refinery and on to another town, probably Peronne, which had been in the French sector. This seemed fairly intact and had not suffered such damage as the other villages. We turned here and made our way back along the road to our camp.

The weather was now dry and sunny, and the sector very quiet. The country was flat and featureless for miles around. It was quite a restful period after the hectic times we had recently endured. There were no civilians and of course no estaminets. We heard that a consignment of rabbits had arrived from Australia and we looked forward to a welcome change of diet, but on examination these proved to be about the size of small starved rats. They were boiled and served up, but found practically useless as food, there being hardly any flesh on the bones.

One day it was our turn to march a few miles to a small village which we found to be surprisingly picturesque and green, with a small stream running by. Here was a corrugated iron shed fitted with an overhead tank and piping as shower baths, the water being pumped from the stream. To our annoyance the pump had broken down; only a few drips of water could be coaxed from the tank. We did, however, get some compensation, as on the way back we discovered a large bed of watercress in the stream, which we gathered and took back to share with other companions. It was rare indeed to get a change from our army rations – never fresh green stuff or fruit.

The village, like a good deal of the land on this sector had been evacuated without fighting by the Germans when they retired to new and strong positions in their rear. These new positions were sited on higher ground, giving them good observation over our trenches on the plains below, thus counteracting much of the advantage we had gained on the Somme by reaching higher ground overlooking Bapaume and Le Transloy and the vast plain beyond, which we were now occupying.

I think it was about this time when leave was given to chaps with longest overseas service, to spend a week at the seaside town of Etaples, with additional pay to spend during the holiday. As I was senior soldier in my section I should have obtained this privilege. I was, however, outside the hut doing a job of sign painting when our Sergeant entered with the pass and gave it to another man, Harry Kay. I was very annoyed when I learned what had happened. However, Harry seemed so pleased with himself that I did not have the heart to press my claim and disappoint him. Also, although the holiday would have made a wonderful break, I would have hated to enjoy a privilege which the others could not share, and in fact I had no great longing to go, having resigned myself to what now seemed inevitable. Somehow I do not think he enjoyed his holiday very much as he was very silent about it on his return, although he may have felt rather guilty about accepting it.

I think the sergeant deliberately passed me over from personal spite, as I sensed that he disliked me. At one time he would send for one of us to clean his boots and equipment. One morning he sent for me. I reported to his tent and found that although it was long past reveille and we had already breakfasted, he was still lying in his blankets, along with his cronies, the sergeant cobbler and sergeant tailor. He told me to clean his equipment but I flatly refused to do so, telling him to get someone else to do his chores. He was rather taken aback and said nothing more, knowing that he was breaking regulations, for not only was he lying in bed long after reveille, but sergeants were not allowed batmen. He never showed open resentment to me afterwards, but I felt that he was only waiting the opportunity to get his own back.

The fellow Harry Kay was a black-haired gypsy-like rogue, a tinker by trade, who I am sure would be delighted by this description. Nothing was safe from his fingers and he would get up to all sorts of escapades. He had plenty of grit when required and would take unnecessary risks to obtain anything he or our section wanted. Surprisingly he and I had a natural affinity to each other, opposite types as we were, and often got into some piece of mischief together. He was some years older than me. I seemed to be the only one with any sort of influence over him; whenever anyone missed some personal item from his haversack I immediately suspected Harry and after saying, 'Come on Harry, hand it over' he would, after a sheepish denial, eventually return the missing article to its rightful owner. When opportunity occurred and funds permitted, we would go on a real 'binge' together, sometimes walking miles to visit a distant estaminet and sample its French beer, usually very poor stuff.

My chief friend and companion however was Dick Sweet, a sturdy young man of about my own age and size, perhaps a little heavier. We would share our food and sometimes our money when one was short of cash, which was most times. Once we carried half a sandbag of sugar we found on the battlefield until the rain dissolved it, our clothing becoming permeated with sweet, sticky mud. At another time we found a half jar of rum and Dick filled his water-bottle with the potent liquid, mixing it with the stale and heavily chlorinated water from mine. We would make porridge with smashed up army biscuits, using a trenching tool handle and a filthy khaki handkerchief to pulverize them, boiling or heating the result in a mess-tin with sugar if available.

On cold wet nights in the open we would sleep together on the soaking mud, using one groundsheet under and one over us, mainly all to no purpose, as it was generally impossible to keep dry.

I find that my memory of events and places after leaving Bapaume sector are very vague and disjointed. We served on many different sectors in and about Arras and having no access to maps, some of the places were only meaningless names to me and to my companions. Sometimes we were in more or less peaceful villages and amongst a few civilians once again; sometimes forward on ground that had only recently been fought over, and thus devoid of buildings and certainly miles from civilization; often in the open or in camps situated in country that was flat and desert-like, with a few roads or sleeper tracks traversing the wasteland. I remember we were at Fremicourt and Lagnicourt and took part in the Battle of Cambrai in November 1917, returning to the Arras front in December.

I will take this opportunity to diverge a little here and deal with oddments and generalities that come to mind. For instance evidence of the artistic ability shown by some of the French soldiers which we came across now and again, particularly around Arras and on the Somme. These were examples of skilful little sculptures left in the dug-outs and shelters. These were cut from blocks of chalk dug from the ground. Also many brass shell cases finely engraved, for use as vases. A few of the British were also very apt at engraving on brass. Here and there one would come across clever figure drawings in black chalk on the white walls of cottages. British efforts were mostly confined to rude messages or rhymes.

Singing was a very popular pastime, especially on the rare occasions when there happened to be a piano available in an estaminet. We would sing at almost any time on the march, in billets or estaminets and sometimes in the trenches. There would be popular sentimental songs of the time, or ribald ones, including "Keep the Home Fires Burning', 'Pack up your Troubles', 'Roses are Blooming in Picardy', 'Tipperary', 'Every Cloud has a Silver Lining', and the coarser variety such as 'Mademoiselle from Armentières', 'Landlord have you a daughter fair', 'Whiter than the Whitewash on the Wall' and a crude parody on 'Sinbad the Sailor Man'. French soldiers would sing 'The Marsellaise' 'Madeleine', 'Alouette' and such songs with much patriotic fervour, especially after a few drinks.

It was noticeable that the Frenchman would always buy his own drinks, unlike the British who would stand treat in turns. This may have been because the French soldier only drew about a half-penny a day in pay, so was always very hard up. When on leave in England we found that treating in pubs was forbidden, although this ruling was largely ignored.

In the villages we noticed that the local postman would make his deliveries by bicycle, blowing a little horn from time to time.

If near a *boulangerie* we could sometimes buy a loaf of the deliciously light French bread, which made a welcome change from our own doughy ration, but this had to be consumed on the day it was purchased, as it would become sour and stale by the following day. Some of the farms made delicious white butter, but could only very rarely be purchased from them. Probably it was illegal for them to sell it to us. The beer was usually very poor and weak, the red or white wine being much more popular with us.

When on the Somme we sometimes saw a French soldier taking rations to the trenches. He would have a number of round flat loaves with the normal hole in the centre, a string threaded through the holes and slung over one shoulder, about a dozen water-bottles containing the red wine issue suspended from the other. We envied them their wine. Generally our bread was quite good if not soaked through or smashed up in transit, being carried in sand bags. Sometimes however it was just a hard pellet of dough, no doubt due to lack of yeast. We would gather round and watch closely as our NCO's cut the loaves into portions, to see that we got a fair share. At times our rations were very meagre, but after heavy casualties there would be plenty for all. We would, however, think of our missing comrades whose food we were now sharing.

When in rest areas we would usually get bacon and sometimes fresh meat stewed with onions and potatoes, but never green vegetables or fresh fruit. Sometimes the meal would be bullybeef, or tinned 'Machonochie' (tinned meat and vegetables) which would not be very palatable when eaten cold. At other times the main meal would be a tin of baked beans containing a minute cube of pork fat. 'Afters' would be boiled rice with condensed milk and sugar. We also had tinned butter, cheese and plum-and-apple jam. There was never fish. On very rare occasions if we were near a canteen we could buy a tin of pilchards or sardines. This all sounds no doubt quite a lavish amount, but it was seldom that we got more than a few of these items at any one time and indeed were lucky to get any when in a difficult part of the line, except perhaps for a couple of very hard biscuits, which must have been dog's biscuits. In fact some of them actually bore the name 'Spratts' indented on them. I think I cracked one or two back teeth on these.

Our water always tasted strongly of chlorine and often of petrol. A rare tot of rum would sometimes be issued, and in the summer a lot of limejuice which as I mentioned earlier the Indian troops would not drink, as they believed it would destroy their virility.

A parcel from home would be received with delight, some of the contents usually being shared with close companions. When the post corporal visited each company with letters and parcels the men would stand around eagerly, hoping to hear their names called, and it was sad to see some of the unlucky ones turning away with disappointment so evident on their faces. The news from home was of course not always good. I remember when Dick Sweet heard of his father's death. Two of us took a long walk with him in silence that evening.

At one village the section was billeted in a stable in the yard of a farm-cum-estaminet. A small dark Frenchman came along one day to kill one of the pigs, and asked for one of us to holds its legs. The other chaps were loath to do this, even Harry Kay. Not liking the thought of an Englishman looking squeamish in front of a foreigner, I volunteered to do this, and was amazed at the speed and skill shown by this man. One quick stab through the side of the neck, and the animal was killed instantly with only a slight shudder. It was then tied to a ladder, singed with a paper torch and opened up in a matter of minutes.

In the evening we went into the estaminet for a drink, and instead of departing by the front door, followed the corporal through the kitchen, where the various parts of the animal were laid out neatly on the table, looking very tempting. The corporal and Harry quickly grabbed enough pork chops for all of us, which we cooked on our coke fire drum and devoured with relish. There were no complaints from the landlord, but the smell of our cooking must have been obvious.

In one corner of the stable was a round pool. We were sleeping on wire beds. I woke in the night feeling that something queer was going on, and lit a candle. The whole floor seemed to be moving. There were thousands of blackish-grey creatures, somewhat resembling tadpoles, advancing over the floor, but on seeing the candle-light they turned and rapidly disappeared into the pool. I do not know what they were, but once saw a few similar creatures come up in a bucket of water from a well. The medical orderly came along next day and put something in the puddle after which we did not see these creatures again.

There was a tub full of German 'stick bombs' known as 'Tater Mashers' in this stable. These were shaped somewhat like a baked bean tin with a wooden handle and a button ended cord for triggering off the detonator. Harry Kay tried out one of these, but it did not explode, probably not having been fused. He took it away and opened it with a chisel, emptying the contents. We kept it as a souvenir. This was typical of Kay's recklessness.

We had a professional lightweight boxer in the battalion, Fred Preston, who said he was a relation of the well-known sporting personality, Harry Preston of Brighton. There was also a good amateur welter-weight in the Machine Gun Company. Our officers put up a purse of 200 francs for a 15 round bout between these two. Preston was a pleasant looking and mild spoken fellow, who however threatened all kinds of mayhem and murder during training. His opponent was a dark, dour looking chap. A proper boxing ring was brought from Divisional head-quarters and erected in the open, with ringside seats for the officers. Although I have seen hundreds of bouts since, this was one of the most exciting I have ever experienced. They were equally clever boxers and fighters. In the 14th round they stood toe to toe, both utterly exhausted, not a pin to choose between them, when a last feeble blow dropped Preston to the boards. His opponent stood over him for a second and then collapsed on top of him. They were both out, and had to be carried from the ring. Several of us climbed into the ring afterwards and found a tooth on the blood spattered canvas. Preston was killed shortly after this.

While in the trenches on the Lagnicourt sector we were visited several times at night by a dog from the German lines. He would arrive over no-man's-land in the evening and go back before dawn. He was a kind of Alsatian, probably what is known as a German police dog, very friendly and he enjoyed sharing our rations. He even visited the support lines.

One day an English airman was shot down in no-man's-land, being brought in by two of our NCO's bearing a white flag. Colonel Shaw and Captain Heath were both wounded by a sniper while directing the rescue. The plane was later dismantled and destroyed by the Royal Engineers.

The London Scottish were raided here by the enemy and lost two men taken prisoners.

In November we heard that we were to take part in an attempt to break through on a wide front of about eight miles and to capture Cambrai, several miles beyond the Hindenburg Line and the Canal du Nord.

About this time we had a flood of pink leaflets sent over by small balloons from the German lines. These caused much amusement as they were printed in French exhorting us to lay down our arms and surrender. I wish I had kept one of these as a souvenir. The enemy would have ben furious had they known to what use they were put.

One day while in camp at Fremicourt we received about 40 wooden sleepers to each of which were attached about half a dozen waist high figures made of wire and canvas, representing infantrymen complete with helmets. Several of us were engaged in daubing them with roughly painted features and buttons. Several waggons passed by containing roughly made wooden and canvas models of tanks. These were to be placed in no-man's-land overnight to act as decoys when the attack commenced. They were constructed so that they could be raised and lowered by strings from the front line trench to represent troops advancing by sections. Two of our brigades were on the extreme left of the attack, our brigade being in reserve.

Dawn broke with a heavy mist. There was no preliminary bombardment this time and the enemy were taken completely by surprise. The assault was at once a success; the infantry following the tanks into and over the Hindenburg Line. The dummy men and tanks, only half visible in the mist, drew much of the German fire away from the assault on the right, until the hoax was discovered, the dummies having caught fire, but they had achieved their purpose at the vital time.

The battalion now took over positions in and about Bourlon Wood and the captured Hindenburg Line, the enemy occupying their support lines and some of the communication trenches connecting these two systems, bombing blocks being established in the latter. In many cases the opposing troops were very close, only about 40 or 50 yards apart and in one or two places only about 20 yards, and could be heard talking. The opposing troops sometimes shouted greetings to each other. As so often the Germans would know the name of the battalions opposing them. They would shout in English during 'stand-to' calling 'Good morning Kensingtons'.

The captured German dug-outs were remarkably well constructed and evidently intended for a lengthy occupation. They were very comfortable, being furnished from the spoils of adjacent villages. Some even had wood panelling and wallpaper. Our men, however were not allowed to use these, the entrances, facing the wrong way for us, being too vulnerable to shell-fire or mortar fire. This however was fairly light owing to the close proximity of the opposing trenches and the danger of shelling one's own men. Action was mostly confined to attempts at bombing along the trenches at certain points, with also a little trench mortar and rifle grenade fire.

During one enemy assault several of our bombing blocks were shelled by our own artillery, causing many casualties, until messages could eventually be got through asking the artillery to lengthen their range. Apart from these organised assaults both sides very sensibly did little to provoke their opponents, which would otherwise entail immediate and precisely aimed retaliation. It was a case of 'live and let live'.

Several of us pioneers were sent up with band saws to cut through a thick tree trunk lying across the top of the front line trench, being a hazard to those passing along the trench at night. It was, fortunately for us, abandoned at the last minute, as the operation would certainly have been heard, if not seen, by the Jerries who were only about 20 or 30 yards away, and would have brought down prompt catastrophe on our heads. It was eventually removed with an explosive charge. Proceeding along the trench a mortar bomb exploded ahead and we heard the ominous and customary shouts for 'stretcher bearers'. Rounding the traverse we saw an NCO sitting propped up against the trench side, his hands pressed to the ground trying to keep his body off the ground and staring with a dreadful puzzled look at the place where his legs should have been. We were glad to get back to the comparatively quieter quarters in support.

The nightly carrying parties here were fairly short, as the transport limbers and pack-horses were able to bring supplies up over generally good routes and well up near to the support lines.

The preliminary attack had been highly successful along the eight mile front on the right, not only overruning the Hindenburg Line and the Canal du Nord (which the Engineers bridged), but on to the outskirts of Cambrai. The cavalry for once made a successful breakthrough. Unfortunately our High Command had not foreseen the possibilities opened up, and had not provided sufficient reserves to turn the operation into a very much greater breakthrough. After a few days the initial impetus came to a standstill and the enemy had gained time to call up reserves and prepare to counter attack. This they did, driving back our forces and regaining ground for several miles back on our right. The attack was held on our sector, Bourlon Wood, in spite of heavy assaults on our positions. Attempts were then made by the enemy to drive back the flanks of the salient and destroy or capture our divisions, but in spite of strong assaults, penetrating into our front line at one or two points, they were driven out and the ground held and consolidated.

At the end of November we were relieved by the Gordon Highlanders and Black Watch, going into reserve camps at Roclincourt and near Arras on the Lens-Arras Road.

From now on the battalion was moved from front to front and I find it quite impossible to remember all but a very confusing number of episodes. Often I and my companions did not know in what particular sector we were, having a very vague idea of the battlefield as a whole. I must ask you therefore to bear with me, as this narrative deals only with my personal memories, and if a detailed description of the various engagements is required, must refer you to whatever historical or official record may be available.

In December we moved to Bailleul and to the Oppy sector south of Vimy Ridge. The main line here was called the Red Line and forward of this was a series of communication trenches leading to a number of isolated outposts. We expected to spend Xmas in the line, but to our delight were relieved a few days before and went back to Roclincourt Camp and the comfort of the huts.

There was now a heavy snow-fall, thus adding to the atmosphere of the season. The battalion was fortunate in now having three of its four Christmases out of the line.

Oh! Oh! Oh! what a lovely war,
Oh! Oh! Oh! what a lovely war,
What do we want with eggs and ham
When we've got plum and apple jam,
As soon as reveille has gone
Our hearts are as heavy as lead
We won't get up till the Sergeant brings
  Our breakfast up in bed.
Oh! Oh! Oh! what a lovely war
Oh! Oh! Oh! what a lovely war
Form fours, Right turn
How can we spend the money we earn?
Oh! Oh! Oh! what a lovely war.

Our pioneer section occupied a fairly large corrugated iron hut fitted with wire bunks, a long table made from a few boxes and planks, with boxes for seats. As the officers' servants were taking their mess-cart to the large YMCA canteen at Arras for their Christmas supplies, we persuaded them to bring us two cases of port wine, some Vermouth and to lend us a dozen glass tumblers. The cooks did an excellent job and conjured up a large roast dinner of turkey, vegetables and Christmas pudding. Every man was given a small Bible from the Queen. These came in useful later as cigarette papers. We also managed to get a few Dutch cigars. We settled down at our table after dinner, with tumblers full of port, plenty of bread, cheese and pickles, and naturally all got very jolly. The QM stores cook came in to greet us. He was a small tubby little fellow, formerly from the Bantam regiment, who when in the wet and mud of the Somme, before getting his present job, would cause us amusement by saying mournfully 'If only my muvver could see me now'. We gave him a drink and he stood at the foot of the table, singing one of his favourite songs, 'Beer, Beer, glorious

Beer' and as he got to the line 'Down by the side of it I'm always willing to lie', Harry Kay hurled a loaf from the far end of the table catching the poor fellow full in the face, causing him to collapse onto the floor. This was a particularly nasty thing to do, and the Corporal grabbed Harry, swinging him at arms length above his head and threw him crashing into the corner onto a heap of empty port bottles, some of which broke, fortunately not harming Harry, who was pretty intoxicated by now.

I went outside in the snow to clear my head a little. Outside was a box on each side of the door, on one of which stood a basin full of dirty water. I attempted to sit on the empty box, but somehow sat down in the basin of water on the opposite side. Getting up I reached for the door, but it was just out of arm's reach, and try as I could was unable to go forward, tipping back on my heels as I stretched forward. Someone heard my shout and hauled me back inside. Harry had now revived and was pumelling a small chap named Swallow, who was helplessly lying back on his bunk. I managed to drag Harry off and separate them.

The next morning I sat on the side of a huge shell-hole outside the hut. The hole was full of snow, at which I sat gazing, trying to clear my head. I discovered that large tumblers full of port wine played havoc with the constitution, and I did not get rid of my hang-over for about a week, when I was detailed for my leave home – the second leave, the date being 1st January 1918. About a half-dozen of us were taken by lorry to a railhead and entrained for Boulogne. I had waited about 14 months for this second leave, which was for 14 days. I remember chatting in the train with a Canadian soldier, who gave me a pipeful of his Canadian tobacco, which I found very pleasant, and he showed me a good method of filling my pipe.

We spent the night in the camp above Boulogne. It was very cold, and I was glad of the tot of rum which I had saved in the silver flask my father had given me the previous year, and strolled about talking with another chap, who like myself had neither the inclination nor the cash to go into the town as most others did for the evening. In the morning we were given a large tub of hot water and soap and after bathing, a complete set of new underwear, so managed with luck to get rid of our vermin before embarking for

England. Before leaving an NCO mounted a table and warned us that if we were discovered taking home any weapons as souvenirs we would have our leave cancelled. I had concealed in my pack and about my person, a fine collection, including a French bayonet, two German bayonets, one being a saw-edged pioneers bayonet, a German stick bomb (defused of course) and the bolt of a German sniper's rifle. Not wishing to risk losing my leave, I disposed of these in the loo, which I regretted later, as so far as I could see no one was searched, and I saw several chaps actually carrying what were no doubt German rifles, wrapped in cloth.

Arriving at Waterloo Station, or was it Victoria, I forget which, I said farewell to my companions, who at my suggestion solemnly agreed to take a day extra. The weather was very foggy and when I got out at Stroud Green Station there was a real London pea-soup fog, and I could not even see the street light outside the station. My parents had now moved to a house in Ridge Road, Hornsey, and I had no idea how to find my way to this strange address in the fog. Fortunately a boy came by and he kindly guided me up the hill and to the house. I mounted the steps to the front door, realizing that it was 2nd January and my 21st birthday. As I knocked the door I remembered the song 'I'm twenty one today', but I had *not* got the key of the door.

My parents and sister were at home, having been advised of my leave, but not knowing the precise day and time for my arrival. It was marvellous to see them again after what seemed an eternity. In fact it was generally agreed that a year in France seemed more like ten years. They were naturally eager to hear of my experiences, but I am afraid I was able to give only a vague and jumbled account with much repetition. My recent experiences had been so many and events followed each other so rapidly, that it was years before I was able to memorize things in a more orderly fashion. Before retiring that night I kissed my father on his forehead as I had always done in the past. I think he was slightly surprised, but not displeased. My mother was greatly distressed when she once again discovered me sleeping on the bedroom floor in the morning.

My mother and I made various visits to see relatives and friends, and one evening we took my father to the Finsbury Park Cinema, his first experience of moving pictures, where we saw a Charlie

Chaplin film. My father did not seem very impressed and was disgusted at the antics of this comedian, which seemed hilariously funny to me and quite innocuous. On the morning of my departure I preferred to say farewell at the door and go off to the station alone. I had a foreboding that this would be my last leave and that if I did indeed return home it would be on a stretcher. I had been very lucky so far, so many of our fellows had been killed or wounded, very few of the original members of the regiment being left. Luck could not hold out much longer, as events were soon to prove. I had a bad omen at Finsbury Park Station. Striding proudly down the sloping subway which was busy with office workers hurrying along to catch their trains, my steel studded boots slipped on the concrete and I fell on my back with a loud crash, loaded down with my pack, equipment, rifle and steel helmet. I felt terribly humiliated at this indignity and am afraid was very rude and abrupt to those good citizens who rushed to help me up.

Our party, the half-dozen who had promised to steal the extra days leave, met at Victoria Station and with hundreds of others, many of whom were bidding farewell to their friends and relatives, entrained for Dover and the boat to Boulogne. Here we spent the night in camp, being sorted out in the morning and despatched to our various units – we getting back to camp on the Lens-Arras Road a few miles beyond the city. Every night we would see and hear revellers returning from a convivial evening in Arras, singing and shouting and sometimes dragging a tipsy comrade along on his heels.

We were soon once again sent further north towards the Bailleul district and on to the Oppy and Vimy Ridge fronts. I can clearly recall one particularly arduous march of some miles over roads and rough sleeper tracks during the night. The route was hard going along the waterlogged and muddy road, much cut up by shell fire. Long lines of horse drawn guns, limbers and waggons were constantly passing, causing us often to step off the track as the wheels of these vehicles would catch one end of a sleeper, many of which were actually floating in mud and water, swinging it round knee high, across the track, threatening a broken leg. Many guns and limbers were stuck in muddy shell-holes, horses and men striving furiously to get them free.

As we got nearer the line the ground ahead was lit up with hundreds of shell flashes and red and green star shells and the whitish illumination of very lights and shrapnel in the sky around us. We realized that we were in a dangerous salient, with shelling coming from front and sides. Large numbers of walking wounded were struggling past us, many muttering the customary 'Good Luck Chum', and telling us that it was hell up the line, and that Jerry was on the offensive. The prospects were far from cheerful, especially after our spell of rest. I once more felt that dreadful sick, empty feeling at the pit of my stomach, known as 'wind up'. It was very like a visit to the dentist, only a hundred times worse.

We reached our destination at dawn, by the track-side, in open plain. Occasional shells seemed to be coming from all directions, and we learned that the enemy were trying to break through at both sides of the salient and to trap us. This position was near Oppy and what was known as the Red Line. I am not sure to this day. Our companies went off ahead later in the day, our section being left by the track side. Many wounded were still coming down, some on limbers and lorries, many walking, some hobbling along with leg wounds, others with bandaged head or limbs. We would occasionally help one on to the back of a passing vehicle when space was available.

Our companies took over the Red Line, which had been strengthened, in support, and then passed forward to the front line in the old Hindenburg Line and to outpost positions in shell holes and trenches beyond. Here the brigade withstood several vicious attacks in an enemy endeavour to recapture the Red Line and retake Vimy Ridge. These attacks were beaten off by our two divisions which we learned later had actually been assaulted by no less than five German divisions. The front line was penetrated in places, but were held up by counter attacks; but the front positions were becoming so smashed up that a short withdrawal was eventually made to the Red Line, where a strong defensive position had now been prepared.

The German dug-outs in this part of the Hindenburg system had been made very comfortable by the enemy, with tables and other furniture filched from the villages.

At the beginning of February we were again in the Red Line.

The weather was now very cold and frosty. The area was subjected to a good deal of gas shelling, the gas being held in the frosty ground, which on thawing out released gas fumes causing many casualties. One day we were resting beside a field dressing station a short distance behind the line, a duck-board track running to the dressing station tent. Groups of men were stumbling blindly along this track with bandaged eyes, led by medical orderlies, each man holding on to the shoulder of the man in front – a case of the 'blind leading the blind', reminiscent of the well known picture by the Flemish artist, Peter Breughel. The artist John Sargent has painted this scene entitled 'Gas'. It is a remarkable painting and so exactly as seen by me that I think the artist must have witnessed this very same incident, possibly taking a photograph for detail. It even shows the wounded and gassed men who were lying about on stretchers awaiting attention or ambulances.

I would like to mention here how irksome was the wearing of our cumbersome gas masks. This was worn in the alert position on our chests, not only restricting our breathing, but inducing perspiration and causing a great decrease in mobility, serious enough as it was when added to the rest of our heavy equipment. Its position on the chest was no doubt decreed by some ignoramus in a comfortable Whitehall office. If he gets to purgatory I hope he will be sentenced to wear a gas mask for eternity. There was more common sense used after the war, when the mask was slung on top of the pack except when a gas alert was in operation.

During one of our periods back at a rest camp we were given another inoculation, and as we lined up for our turn with the doctor's needle, several men actually fainted. After what they had been going through it seemed surprising to see men passing out from fear of a tiny needle prick.

One day the doctor offered to pull teeth if required. I had recently been troubled with a back molar, no doubt cracked while dealing with our hard dog's biscuits, so lined up in the barn for my turn. There was an upturned tub to serve as dentists' chair, and our small doctor flourishing his one and only huge pair of forceps, evidently enjoying his gruesome pastime. There was no anaesthetic, and the victims seemed to be suffering greatly from his ministrations. One after another prospective patient was quietly slipping away, myself included. I am glad to say my toothache disappeared, not to return until after the war.

From time to time a man would have to be sent away with shell-shock, his nerve having broken down under the strain of warfare, close proximity to an explosion, or even having been buried alive.

After one rather trying tour in the trenches, we came back to a quiet village and one chap chose this opportunity to desert and hid in a nearby wood. After a day or two he was caught and condemned to death. A small tin lid was handed to me to paint white. The firing party marched off next morning, the tin disc fixed to his chest, and he was shot. The sentence seems very savage, but was customary, as desertion or cowardice has to be dealt with drastically in warfare, not only to discourage waverers, but to prevent the spread of panic. In this case the sentence was very drastic, as the offence was not actually committed 'in the face of the enemy'. In fact he may even have got away with shell-shock if he had disappeared during battle.

I remember that at Arras during the previous year a man was brought back to the battalion from London. He was one of two men who deserted early in 1915 and managed to get back to England, but he would not say, only telling me that the authorities were very curious to find how he had accomplished this, and he had given them the information in return for his life. Military Police would carry out spot checks in pubs and cinemas in England to try and discover any deserters. They had caught him asleep in bed one night.

We had several cases of self-inflicted wounds. For instance, there was the transport man who had deliberately crushed his foot under a waggon wheel on the Somme. Two men cut their hands badly on opening bully beef tins at Arras. Another man, who later became a well-known war artist, was reputed to have shot himself through the foot; this was a well known way of getting invalided out, but the boot would show burn marks from the rifle muzzle, so some cunning culprits would fire through a sandbag placed over the foot. Another trick was to hold a hand up above the parapet, hoping to get it shot by a sniper. Then there were men who would keep whacking their knee-cap with a wet towel to induce a synovitis knee. Chewing cordite was said to cause a rise in temperature, simulating fever. Others were very clever at pretending deafness, but were mostly detected fairly easily by doctors tricking them into a mistake. I heard of one man who although suspected by the doctors of malingering, could not be caught out, until sent to the railway station, accompanied by a medical orderly, ostensibly to go to London for his discharge. As the man entered the railway carriage the orderly suddenly asked if he had his railway ticket. The fellow was so jubilated at the thought of getting away that he carelessly said, 'Yes'.

As regards genuine illnesses, the most usual would be the mysterious ailment called trench-fever, trench-feet and scabies, the latter usually caused by lice. Boils were very prevalent, no doubt due to lack of green stuff and overmuch tinned meat. It was not worthwhile going on sick parade for minor ailments such as colds, influenza, and so on, as these merited little or no consideration, the only remedy given for almost any complaint being the notorious 'Number Nine' pill – which we believed this pill to be the only medicine available to our doctors.

We spent a few days in the line at Vimy Ridge, taking over from the Canadians who had made themselves famous by its capture. Our section were in a support line in old broken down trenches just below the top of the ridge, which was quite bare and pitted with shell-holes. I would like to have got a view of the enemy side of the ridge, but as the ground in front was so open and deserted I could not make myself too conspicuous by wandering off on my own up the hundred yards to the top. We had a thoroughly miserable few days and nights; the ground was wet and muddy and entirely without shelter of any kind – we had no rations and no water, but some of us chanced making tea with water from the bottom of the trench, much befouled as it was. It was difficult to get the water anywhere near hot, as we only had old letters and envelopes and whatever scraps of wet timber we could find lying around.

We had a surprise visit by the Brigadier General, who came just at the back of me and said to us, 'Never mind, you will soon be relieved', after which he and his party hurried back again to the rear. We noticed that he did not go further forward than our support line, and showed no inclination to take a look over the top of the ridge. However, 'his word was as good as his bond,' and we were relieved later in the day and marched back to a reserve camp near Arras.

The Corporal and half a dozen of us obtained a day's leave in Arras, managed to get a lift in a lorry. Quite a number of civilians had now returned to the city, and several shops and estaminets had opened up. We had quite an enjoyable day including a meal of eggs and chips, plenty of white wine, and actually found a French photographer in business. We took the opportunity of having a group photograph taken, a really first class effort, I still have a couple of copies, the prints being ready before our return.

The streets in the busy part were packed with troops of many different regiments, including English, Scots, Welsh, Irish, Canadians, Australians, New Zealanders and South Africans. Away from the shopping areas the rest of the streets and squares were almost deserted. In the middle of one large deserted square, was a garden seat under a group of trees. Reclining on the seat was a Scottish soldier, apparently getting over a debauch. He was busily searching himself for pests, at the same time solving once and for all the interesting problem of what the Scots wore under their kilts. We had no transport back to camp, so commenced our long tramp over the fields, fortifying ourselves on the way with several bottles of wine we had acquired before departure.

We were soon to hear the disquieting news of the collapse of the Russian army and the inevitable release of perhaps a million Germans to reinforce our opponents and enable them to make an enormous assault against the French and ourselves, now much weakened and depleted by our recent efforts. It is true that the Americans were about to enter the war on our side, but only a very small number had so far arrived in France, and it would no doubt be many months before they would be over in any strength; and even so, they would be green and inexperienced in warfare. The question was whether we would be able to last out against the overwhelming numbers and armaments shortly to be thrown against us until the Americans could arrive in strength.

At about this time it was decided to convert our brigade to a three battalion basis instead of the four battalion formation, thus putting our army on the same principle as that of the Germans. This would serve not only to increase the man-power of each battalion, but make possible the formation of extra divisions. This move was received by us with some misgiving, as it would no doubt mean more frequent periods in the front line and less in reserve. There was much speculation and rumour as to which of our battalions would lose its identity, and this eventually turned out to be the Rangers (12th London) thus leaving our brigade composed of the London Scottish, the 4th London (Fusiliers) and ourselves, the Kensingtons. We received about 150 men from the now disbanded Queen Victoria Rifles.

On 21st March the Germans launched their great offensive on a front of about 40 miles, with an enormous force of about 70 divisions. The blow fell where it was least expected and where the line was only thinly held. In about a week the whole of the old Somme battlefield was lost, the enemy attacking in huge masses of men, completely over-running our troops in spite of magnificent efforts to resist. Many of our battalions were completely annihilated within a few hours. The advance was finally halted before Amiens.

The next attack was expected to fall on the Arras front, which now presented a threat to the German flank. Trenches and strong points were prepared hurriedly in the back areas, the strategy now being to fall back gradually to these new positions, hoping that the enemy would eventually become exhausted. Their lines of communication would now be greatly extended and if we could hold out they would have great difficulty in maintaining their supplies as they got further from their bases. Many of our dumps of food and ammunition had to be abandoned and fell into the enemy's hands. It was later found that many of the German troops were dismayed and discouraged to find how well we were supplied with food in comparison with their own meagre rations, and were faced with the proof that their submarine campaign had failed in its attempt to starve us out.

Arras was evacuated of civilians and the huge army canteen established there was abandoned, leaving great masses of food and drink behind. These were of course looted by the large numbers of men of different regiments on their way to the rear, and as may be imagined there was much intoxication among the retreating troops, both from this canteen and many other sources. This state of affairs must have caused much anxiety to our Higher Command, but no doubt the advancing German forces were faced with a similar problem. As far as I know our division took no hand in these debauches, discipline being high, and also that our task was to stand and defend Arras, so had no opportunity or temptation to raid these treasures. We had noticed some time before this that the green fields behind Arras were being hurriedly ploughed in patches, the object of which was obscure, but no doubt intended to assist in ranging for artillery fire, or air observation purposes.

As mentioned, our division was to remain on this front and cover the anticipated enemy attack on Arras. Orders were read out to us from General Haig that we were now to fight with out 'backs to the wall', there was to be no retreat and we were to hold on to the end. The word 'retire' was not to be used, particularly as it was rumoured that Germans disguised as British officers were ordering retirement, thus adding to the confusion.

It is surprising that all ranks were behaving with great coolness and steadfastness. It has always been said that this attitude is typical of the British, who fight best when in a seemingly hopeless situation. I do not think it occurred to any of us that we could ever be defeated, so great was our pride and faith in the strength of the British Empire with all its great traditions. As for myself I now felt completely dedicated to the war and gave up all thought of surviving it. I had no trepidations as to our final victory and felt complete confidence in the determination and steadfastness of my comrades.

While in reserve we were set to work in encircling all huts and tents with shallow trenches. It was usual for all camps to have a Lewis gun mounted on a post, with a gunner in constant attention to deal with any German aeroplane appearing in the vicinity. These planes were now visiting us frequently, evidently for observation purposes.

One day a German plane came swooping down directly towards us as we were standing outside our hut watching its approach, thinking it had been hit and was about to land. It came to within about 50 yards of us and we could plainly distinguish the features of the pilot, when suddenly it shot up and away with its information and probably photographs. For some reason the Lewis gunner was not at his post at the time. Knowing what I do now, I realize that we should have shot at it; it was so near and as it was coming straight towards us would have been impossible to miss. These airmen were remarkably audacious and plucky. We were not trained to deal with them or their wiles.

VII

Blighty – End of Diversion

On 7th April 1918 we were moved to the Beaurains-Tilloy sector, near Telegraph Hill. The Germans were now in possession of Neuville-Vitasse which we had attacked and captured the previous year almost to the day. We took over from the Canadians and South Africans, my section entering the same shallow trench on the ridge immediately to the right of Beaurains, which we had occupied on the eve of our attack twelve months previously. It was night time when we made the relief. The section of South Africans relieved could not get away quick enough and seemed to be in a bad state of nerves, hurrying off without a word to us. They must have had a pretty bad time, although things seemed quiet enough that night, but their attitude did not seem to bode well for our future.

The following day was uneventful until in the late afternoon six of us were ordered to act as a ration party and go back along the road to collect rations and return to Beaurains where we would be met at the old British front line and directed to the company quarter-master's dug-out. The corporal, who should have been in charge as was normal, stayed behind with Harry Kay, and we set off without an NCO. We reached the road where it was decided that I would be in charge, having longest service, although the youngest.

We set off down the road towards Achicourt, finding the pile of rations dumped in a shell hole beside the road. There were two dozen sandbags full and 12 petrol cans of water. We had left our equipment behind, carrying only our loaded rifles, which incidentally never left our hands when in the battle area. Dusk had now set in, and while we were engaged in tying the sandbags in pairs to sling over our shoulders, the enemy commenced shelling along the road we were to traverse. A battery of artillery came by at a tremendous gallop, the four teams of horses tearing along, panic-stricken, eyes bulging and nostrils flaring, the drivers crouched over their animals. I had seen pictures of horses galloping into action, but never thought I would ever see the actual thing. The impression was exactly as pictured by war artists.

The artillery were evidently retiring to positions in the rear to prevent capture. I thought, 'This is it' and felt that the infantry in front were being abandoned to their fate and we would have to bear the brunt of an attack without artillery support. The enemy no doubt had observed the withdrawal and were shelling the road unmercifully. The bombardment continued without pause and I decided it would be as well to carry on with our job and get it over, rather than stay put and probably get hit anyway.

I suggested trying to carry the whole burden in one trip, as although we might with luck get through and back in one go, there seemed little chance of our luck holding out a second time. However, a couple of our shortest chaps said they could not manage the four sandbags and two petrol tins, in addition to their rifles, so I reluctantly agreed to make the two journeys, and we shouldered four sandbags each, which were difficult enough to manage, as they and our rifles would keep slipping from our shoulders. If our hands were also engaged with the petrol tins (two gallons each tin) it would have been decidedly awkward to try and stop everything sliding off every few minutes. It was by now quite dark, except from the light of the bursting shells, falling on each side as well as on the road itself. After some 500 yards we reached the trench where we were met by the look-out and directed to the destination about 100 yards along the trench. We were advised that owing to mud and other obstructions it was easier to go along the top.

We turned left with open ground on one side and trees on the right. We came to a large pit or depression which looked like an old artillery position, no doubt from which the guns we saw on the road had just been withdrawn. We were told to leave our burdens at the entrance to a dug-out, and made our way back onto the road and to the dump. The road was still being shelled, but we got through without mishap, gathered up the petrol cans of water and returned to the trench. It was now very dark indeed and starting to rain, the road still under shell-fire. There was no one now at the trench entrance and we moved along and dumped our burdens as before, meeting a party of our drummers who evidently had been on a similar job.

Suddenly a barrage of shells came screaming over and dropping a short distance beyond us, several bursting quite close. We moved to the trench side, bunching to get down at a convenient place. It is possible after a little experience to tell from the scream of an oncoming shell to know if it is going to fall within a few yards or to pass over one's head. I heard one coming that I knew was going to land on us. I did not hear the final scream of the shell, nor what must have been the awful noise of its explosion. I felt a terrific blow on the left side of my back, like the kick of a horse, felt my knees buckle under me and lost consciousness.

I have no idea for how long I was in this state, but came to with an awful pain in my back and stomach, and hearing a lot of moaning noises. Realising that some of the moaning was coming from me, I shut up, but there was much of it still going on around me.

There was a suffocating feeling in my chest and I had to force my breath in short gasps, each gasp causing much pain. The worst pain was across my stomach and I was reluctant to put my hand there, being sure that my mid-section had been blown away. My feet seemed to be moving up and down, as if on a bicycle, making me think that my spine had been broken causing this reaction.

I tried to kick out to find if I had any control over my legs, and heard a clonk as my boot must have contacted a steel helmet. One source of groaning immediately stopped, as also did the circular motion of my feet, and I realised that some poor fellow must have been grasping my ankles above his head in his agony. I could hear and see the shells still bursting all around.

Now convinced that I was dying I had a peculiar hallucination of a light opening between clouds in the sky and voices singing and calling me in. I was not at all scared during all this, but apart from the pain felt quite calm. After a while I began to think how much I would like to see my mother, father and sister just once again before I died, and then, of all things, a longing to walk once more at night along by Finsbury Park, and became determined that I would last out to do these things.

Another shell came particularly close and I thought how silly to stay here in the open when only a yard or two from the edge of the trench, where now I could hear voices and movements of passers by. There were several calls for help from wounded men lying around, but no one came, and we heard one voice from the trench saying, 'We are all wounded ourselves here.'

Although it was terribly painful, I tried by degrees to inch my way towards the trench by using one elbow, eventually managing to reach the edge, landing on what must have been a corrugated iron shelter. There were voices quietly talking under this, but as my weight was shaking this feeble support the men underneath must have been scared, as their voices stopped.

Several fellows passed, and I tried to call their attention, but they made no effort to help me although within arm's reach. At last two men came by and lifted me down to the bottom of the trench, which was inches deep in mud. The rain was still drizzling down. Just near me was a dug-out entrance, and from the sounds the dug-out steps were full of men, some wounded. I could hear other wounded men lying nearby in the trench. The two fellows were awfully good and stayed with me all night.

There was a young man lying beside me and who was gasping for breath just as I was, but after a while the gasping stopped and I heard someone say he was dead and named him as Drummer Stroud. I was distressed to hear this, as he was a fine, well bred and principled fellow, much liked and respected by all. I at last ventured to place my hand on my stomach and was agreeably surprised to find it still there. There was a wide canvas belt under my tunic and in order to relieve my breathing I tried to unbuckle this, but found that my fingers would not function. One of the fellows undid this for me. There must have been about twenty of us casualties.

I learned that all six of my party had been wounded, but do not know if any had been killed. Several had leg wounds, including my pal Dick Sweet, whom I ran into several years later when visiting the library in Westminster.

Towards dawn stretcher bearers were busy taking away some of the wounded. At day-break an officer came along and said that I was to go next. Some time elapsed before the two stretcher bearers arrived. They said they had been working all night and could not take any more as they were completely exhausted. However, they evetually said they would take just one more, and lifted me onto a stretcher, struggling along the muddy trench. Each time the stretcher was lowered to the ground onto the thick mud, the lumps would press into my back causing intense pain.

As we neared the road we passed under a covered tunnel, causing the bearers to stoop and drag me along the trench bottom. They got me to the roadside. There was still some desultory shelling along the road and several motor ambulances came by driving very fast. They would not stop, probably being full up. The drivers must have been very plucky, evidently going quite close to the front line at the far side of Beaurains.

Eventually one ambulance stopped and I was slid aboard amongst several other casualties, and we set off at a cracking pace towards Achicourt, accompanied by shell-bursts en route and negotiating the many shell-holes in the road. The ambulance entered Achicourt and stopped by a cellar entrance along the main road. Several stretcher cases were taken ahead of me head first. I tried to implore the stretcher bearers to take me down feet first. However, head first I went, and naturally lost consciousness at once.

I came to lying on some sort of table, the cellar in candle-light, and a medical orderly binding up my two hands. I had no idea why, as I had not realized or felt that my hands were damaged. He said there was also a small wound above my left ear, and asked if there was anywhere else. I said my back and stomach. He slit open my tunic and found a wound in my shoulder about the size of a penny.

A cup of water was placed at my lips, but I was only allowed to wet them, thirsty as I was. I found afterwards that my medical card was marked 'Gunshot wounds in hands and stomach'. I was taken up and put into another ambulance and driven off to what turned out to be only one of several dressing stations en route to a railhead.

I was only semi-conscious and must have slept most of the time. One stop was in a huge warehouse or brewery, full of warm water radiators on top of which we were placed on stretchers. There must have been a hundred or more of us. An orderly armed with a large pair of scissors swiftly ripped through my clothing, leaving me like a peeled banana, and wrapped me in a blanket, the contents of my pockets being placed in a cotton bag and tucked in with me. I was then for the first time allowed a tiny sip of tea from a large mug and slid into a converted cattle truck with other stretcher cases. An orderly flung a paper-back novel on my blanket. It was difficult to use my heavily bandaged hands, but I found the book to be a lurid murder story which hardly appealed to me at the time, and anyway I was in too dazed a state to read.

We arrived at Etaples and were taken by motor ambulances to the hospital, a large collection of long wooden huts. I was put into a bed in the South African Ward. There were probably about 20 or so beds in the ward attended by several white South African nurses and a male orderly. Thousands of wounded men were coming down from the line at this time, many being shipped off as quickly as possible to England. These fine dedicated women were working twenty hours a day, but were to be killed a few weeks afterwards as I will relate.

My breathing was now easier but still difficult and I was fairly comfortable in bed so long as I kept perfectly still. My right hand had swollen until it looked like a small football. I had read in a novel about a man who laid on his side in order to keep closed a wound in his chest, so I laid on my left side as much as possible. The only thing I dreaded was the bed-making routine, when the orderly would pick me up, aided by the nurse and hold me stretched out across his arms while the bed was made up. This caused me the most agonizing pain, like lying on a red hot grid-iron and I was forced to clench my teeth in order to stop crying out. They insisted on carrying out this routine in spite of my pleas. I am sure they did not realise the pain they were causing, to say nothing of the damage. It would probably have served me better if I had indeed yelled out. There were two holes in my right hand, each as big as eggcups, on the knuckle part of my forefinger, and a small wound on my left wrist; also a tiny wound on my left temple.

Wounds were uncovered by all in the mornings, when the doctor would make his round of inspections, sometimes attending to bad wounds himself, but mostly leaving the dressings to the nurses and the orderly to see. Many of the wounds were terrible, the ward looking like a butcher shop. Some with amputated arms and legs, the poor fellow opposite having lost both legs, an arm and a hand.

In the next bed to me was a youngster of about 18, whose head was swathed in bandages which, when removed exposed the side of his face, one side of his jaw bone and teeth missing. He seemed remarkably calm and cheerful in spite of this, no doubt having been drugged. No attempt was ever made to screen such casualties. The wounded men were very stoical and only occasionally would a moan be heard, usually from an amputation case. One or two patients passed away in full view of the rest of the ward.

A clergyman visited us one day and offered to write home. I was only half conscious at the time and could say nothing – he suggested sending my love. He looked rather puzzled at my lack of response. I felt too weak to say anything but acquiesce to his suggestion and I think he gave me up as a hopeless job.

Next day I was wheeled into a dark room at the end of the ward. This was the X-ray room, the only light coming from an enormous glass bowl, a pale mauvish light. I was left with the young radiographer, who had great difficulty in lifting me upright in a sitting position on a narrow shelf against a large black screen. Somehow I managed to remain upright for a few seconds, without slipping off, or fainting, while he took the necessary picture. This was, he told me, to determine the level of blood in my lung and to locate the position of the piece of shell or shrapnel.

Next morning two doctors and a nurse arrived with a hand pump, tube and glass jar. The younger doctor proceeded to push what looked like a long knitting needle in behind my shoulder, just below the shoulder blade. He soon said that he could not get it any further and it must be in the scapula, but the elder man said, 'No, go on, push, push.' Then the pumping commenced and I felt suffocating, gasping horribly and fighting for breath. The nurse was holding my hand, and also a glass with something tasting like champagne to give after the ordeal. I could see the jar now three-quarters full of blood, and heard the nurse say a pint and a half. I felt thoroughly exhausted, but soon found it easier to breathe.

The apparatus was known as an aspirator. I understand that nowadays an improved instrument is used which pumps air or oxygen into the lungs to replace the blood and so eliminate the distress caused by the old method.

A new medical card was now fixed to me reading 'Haemothorax: foreign body lies at the head of the seventh rib, partially imbedded in the eighth dorsal vertebrae.'

Soon I was feeling a good deal better and no longer getting blood in my mouth. I had always been a heavy smoker, and there were a few cigarettes in my little cotton bag. I asked the doctor if I could smoke. After thinking a moment he said, 'Yes, if you want to.'

I did, setting light to the large bunch of cotton wool on my bandaged hand. I had the presence of mind to snatch the bandage off, but apparently opened an artery, as the blood spurted from my hand in jerks, several feet distant to the floor. As I stared stupidly at this, one of the patients shouted for help and the orderly came running, stopped the flow and bandaged my hand up tightly again. Not a word was said in reprimand.

After I had been in the ward about ten days the doctor came and asked me if I would like to go to Blighty. Although I did not feel fit enough for such a voyage, I eagerly said yes, and the next day was taken to the docks and slid down a shute to below decks, being very gently handled by sturdy looking German prisoners, actually Prussian Guards, acting as stretcher bearers on the hospital ships. The sea outside the harbour looked very rough and I wondered what would happen if I became sea-sick. Below decks was crammed with hundreds of stretcher cases. I was given a bowl of soup, which must have been drugged, as I went off immediately into a sound sleep, waking up just as we were entering Folkestone Harbour. There I was laid on the station platform and two ladies came to ask if I wanted anything to eat or drink, but went off as soon as they read my label, as also did a man in civilian clothes. I found that in my semi-conscious state I had a feeling of irritation and intolerance towards these well meaning and kindly people, as also in the case of the clergyman at Etaples, wishing only to be left alone. I had probably been doped and found it difficult to respond to their ministrations, although I felt more grateful and at ease with service and medical personnel. A great gap had grown between the service man and the civilian which took years to eradicate. Perhaps one of the most profound things that evolved from the war was the almost unbelievable loyalty and comradeship amongst those who served in the trenches.

We were put onto a hospital train, in charge of a very fierce and masculine matron. We passed through London in the night without stopping, much to my disappointment, and on to Newcastle-under-Lyme, near Stoke. I was taken by motor ambulance from the station to the Stoke War Hospital, actually at Newcastle. It was late at night and I was put into bed and soon a buxom, good looking Irish nurse, young and rosy cheeked, came along and gave me a good sponge over. I felt very embarrassed as I must have been in a filthy state, not having been cleaned up in the busy hospital at Etaples, where things were too hectic for such refinements. I then had my toenails cut, was given a feed and a drink, and fell soundly asleep.

In the morning a young nurse came up to inspect my label and went squealing away excitedly saying, 'Tommy Tucker, we've got Tommy Tucker', other squeals coming from beyond the door. Henceforth I was known as 'Tommy', a nickname I did not appreciate. However, 'Tommy' it remained. In France I was called 'Tuck'.

My back and ribs still felt painfully bruised, but it was not so bad if I kept still. My right fist was like a bandaged football and there was a small bandage on my left wrist. After a day or two I taught myself to write with my left hand. At first the letters were huge with a strong tendency to write backwards, but soon I was able to manage tolerably well. I now have an example in the congratulatory letter I sent to my cousin Betty Thring on her marriage to Major Strubbe of the Canadian Engineers.

How peaceful and relaxing was this life. Here I was to lie, eventually to sit up, for about six weeks. The hospital, set in neat grounds surrounded by a high wall, was originally the Stoke Workhouse. It was a group of very modern brick wards. My ward was a light, high ceilinged room, holding probably about 16 or 18 beds. The walls were dove grey distempered with white woodwork and a highly polished pine-wood floor. The iron bedsteads were covered with very clean white counterpanes, which the nurses would fuss over almost each time they passed, tucking in and smoothing out. The ward was kept immaculately clean, as were the wash and bathrooms. Patients had to mind their step, the floors being so highly polished. I came to grief, slipping on to my back shortly after I was well enough to walk about. On the right of each bed was a small white cupboard. Very large windows ran along the wall on my side of the ward, giving an excellent light for reading.

Matron was a very stern looking and strict little woman; nurses and patients alike treated her with awe and instant obedience. There were four or five nurses, all very nice young girls. My nurse was the rosy cheeked Irish girl named Nurse Callan who had first attended me. She was about 24 years old, high complexioned and roundish, good looking face – a very capable type and well educated. I seemed to be her favourite patient, getting most of her attention and the best of the bowls of flowers. My only complaint was that she would suddenly pinch my toe in a most cruel manner, making me very cross, as I did not feel up to such treatment at the time.

I heard from my mother and father, whose letter in beautiful copperplate writing I still have. They had received an official telegram to the effect that I had been dangerously wounded. My mother obtained a pass and came to see me twice, getting a bedroom in the village overnight.

The ward cleaner was a dear old soul, very Irish, small and bubbling over with cheeriness. I think she really loved us all and would regale us while polishing the floor with her two songs, 'When Irish Eyes are Smiling' and 'Tipperary'. She would do anything for us, bringing in things from the shops, such as cigarettes, chocolate and stationery.

In the bed on my left was a young chap with his knee-cap shot off. On the right another boy with a small round shrapnel wound in the cheek of his posterior, causing some amusement when he laid on his face exposing his embarrassing wound to the nurse for the daily dressing. There were a few amputation cases and a very badly scalded man, also a rather nasty gas casualty, grossly swollen and inflamed. We were all surprisingly cheerful and friendly. It is a curious thing, but I have generally found that beyond saying what unit we had served with, little or no mention was made of our experiences; in fact I think we had put them in the back of our minds. I also found the same thing after the war. One lively youngster swore he would never be sent out again. He had a damaged knee, and after the morning inspection when the ward was clear of nurses, he would get out of bed and dance about with his swollen knee, which must have been painful, bashing it with his wet towel in order to simulate a synovitis knee.

After about a month I was placed on a stretcher and taken across the yard to the X-ray room, where a young radiographer examined my back under X-ray and pencilled a blue triangle over the position of the shrapnel in my spine. He said this was to locate the position for an operation to remove the foreign body, which was 2½ inches below the surface. However, the doctors decided to let well alone and so there was no operation.

I would like here to pay homage to the radiographers, many of them quite young men who knowingly risked their lives, due to the probability of an early death from prolonged exposure to radiation. Also the doctors, nurses and orderlies, who often worked very long hours in hazardous conditions.

The doctor on his rounds in the morning looked at me in surprise and said, 'You've been out of doors,' and instructed that in future I should be put out in the sunshine every day. Just those few yards in the open air must have had a remarkable effect on my appearance. Thereafter I was taken into the yard on a stretcher for a few hours each day, which must have greatly hastened my recovery. Soon I was able to get up and go to the dining room for meals. It was marvellous when I was strong enough to venture down the hill to the village and back, and after a while was able to walk quite a distance without distress. Our main meal was usually a very small portion of tasteless boiled chicken or fish and boiled rice. I soon developed a healthy appetite and applied for my back pay of several pounds, and with my companion, a Durham miner, would buy a more substantial meal in the village and sometimes a beer at one of the local inns, where we were not supposed to be served. We were dressed in the blue and white hospital clothes – mine were enormous, making me feel very awkward and self-conscious.

One day a few of us were taken over an iron foundry at Stoke; it looked like a fiery hell to me and I was glad to get out again. I could not understand how anyone could spend his life working in the fierce heat and sparks from cauldrons of molten metal passing overhead, tending furnaces and guiding huge red hot girders along with steel poles.

I met a buxom young woman who was employed as cook by one of our doctors. We would go to the cinema in the afternoon, where she would insist on paying her own way, and sit holding hands. I found that she was taking me too seriously, and not being prepared for this and indeed with no prospects for the future, I wrote ending our association, receiving a heart-rending letter in reply. There was a very pretty fair-haired young nurse in the ward and we would flirt rather outrageously. Although strictly forbidden, I took her to tea in the village one afternoon. If caught this would have meant her transference to another hospital, regulations in this regard being very strict. I still have the 'kiss-curl' cut from her forehead with my jack-knife. After my discharge I heard from Nurse Callan that the girl had got a transfer to Charing Cross Hospital in London and suggested that I get in touch with her there, which however I did not bother to do.

There were two sisters, one married, working in the catering department of the hospital. They invited me, with a South African and another patient to their home in Silverdale for tea one Sunday. Their father was a very nice man employed as a colliery fireman. The family gave us a most elaborate high tea, which was quite a feat in wartime. We accepted another invitation for the next Sunday, and much appreciated the courtesy of these kind people.

In the yard outside our ward was a large, open-sided summer house mounted on a turntable. This was occupied by a swarthy and strong looking young man, who nevertheless was supposed to be dying of TB. When the doctor prescribed fresh air treatment for me, the matron moved me into a bed next to this fellow, but next morning, the doctor hearing of this, soon had me removed back to the ward.

This man was a real gypsy – quite a pleasant chap who knew and accepted his fate apparently quite cheerfully. He said he was related to the circus family of Bostock and Wombwell and that his aunt, of whom he spoke with great deference, was a gypsy queen. She arrived one Sunday on a visit to him. A most elegantly dressed and regal looking old lady, driving a beautiful pony and trap, and evidently quite aware of her importance in life.

The patient appeared to be making a recovery and was allowed up and dressed. He would come into the ward and entertain us with tricks, kicking up a cigarette and catching it in his mouth and so on. However, he soon had a relapse and died before I left hospital. He used to pass his time doing fine embroidery work and I sometimes bought coloured silks for him in the village.

Some of the patients were being sent to a convalescent hospital on the Lancashire coast and I was hoping to get my turn. However, I learned that I was to go to Hampstead with a view to getting my discharge from the services. In August I was given a medical check-up and interview by a doctor who pretended he had mislaid my papers. He seemed surprised when I repeated 'verbatim' to him, parrot fashion, the details of my medical report, and asked where I had gained my medical knowledge. He then interrogated me regarding the locality in which I was wounded, but could not find this on his map until I pointed it out to him.

One morning a civilian called for me in his car and chatted up the nurse till long after we should have left, much to my anxiety and annoyance, then drove in a hair-raising and dangerous manner to the station, where I rushed and just caught my train as it was on the move. On arrival in London I found my way to the hospital at Hampstead, a dismal looking place after the one at Newcastle. Here I was again interviewed by a doctor, who also appeared to have lost my papers, and was impressed by my parrot like recital of the medical details. I think that in both cases this was a ruse to test whether I was the right man, as there were so many tricks played by malingerers and dodgers trying to get their discharge dishonestly. However, he showed me an X-ray film of my chest and pointed out the piece of shell embedded in my backbone, saying how lucky I had been as the missile had only missed my heart by a fraction.

Next day I went before a tribunal one young doctor saying that I was experienced in clerical work, or perhaps I could be useful with a broom. He seemed intent on keeping me in the services. His suggestions however were ignored by the others, and my discharge papers signed. I went down to the stores and was fitted out with a very serviceable herring-bone suit and a cloth cap. With a kit bag of belongings on my shoulder I set off joyously for Finsbury Park and thence home, a civilian once more, the date being 22nd August 1918. It was a wonderful feeling being home again with my mother, father and sister. I drew my gratuity of £17, most of which had to be spent on a raincoat, shoes, hat and underwear. I also drew £1 a week subsistence allowance for a month or so. I had to attend the Great Northern Hospital several times a week at Holloway for electric massage for my right-hand and forearm. My right forefinger was useless, hanging down and incapable of movement. I had refused the offer at Newcastle to have it amputated.

A Doctor Rose said that the doctor at Newcastle was a fool, and asked if I would consent to an operation known as a tendon graft, which was then in a rather elementary stage, although he said he could not promise success. I agreed and the operation was carried out, the doctor expressing disappointment with the result. Personally I was delighted, as I could now extend the finger and use it for writing and so on, although it could only be clenched half-way when closing my fist.

In the ward I was given a large dinner and told the operation would not take place until the next day. However, immediately after this heavy meal I was sent up to the operating theatre and put under sedation. I came to in the middle of the night feeling dreadfully sick and being aware of a very painful left thigh. There was a large bandage around the thigh and I had a terrible fright, believing that there had been a mistake and that my leg had been amputated. Furtively I felt below the bandage and found the rest of my leg still there – perhaps the surgeon had realised his error in time and only partially cut off my leg. A nurse presently came along and told me not to worry, as a piece of the silver skin had been removed from a thigh muscle with which to join up the tendon in my right hand. The leg, with a 7 inch incision and 8 stitches, was extremely painful and kept me in bed in hospital for about a week before I was able to walk about. I then left for home with my bandaged hand in a sling until it finally healed. I have a photograph of myself, arm in sling, standing beside my father in the garden.

Before ending treatment at Holloway I had to report to a doctor who I had recognised at once as he who had used the aspirator on my lung at Etaples. He said, 'I've seen you before somewhere, and when I told him, he said he remembered and was surprised to see me looking so fit, asking if I would mind him examining me. I stripped off coat and shirt and he turned to the nurse and told her how wonderful that I had made such a recovery after only a few months. He must have had a phenomenal memory, as he probably attended to hundreds of wounded men a week at the time, and I would have looked a very sorry sight at Etaples. Then he told me that about a week after I left Etaples Hospital, a long range shell destroyed the South African ward, killing all the nurses. This was very sad news to me, as I so much admired the efforts and devotion to duty of these fine women. It had been another and final lucky escape for me.

My cousin Frankie Jones, who had been a sergeant in the Grenadier Guards from Mons onward and was mentioned in despatches several times, had recently taken a commission in a Welsh regiment, gone to Ireland and then back to France. About a week before Armistice Day my Aunt Squib came and told us that Frankie, her stepson, was assumed killed, having gone forward by himself after the retreating Germans and was never seen or heard of again. His father, Uncle Frank, an old Grenadier Guards sergeant and a veteran of the Boer War, had early in the war become a Captain in a Suffolk regiment, was wounded in the head and now discharged. His second son, following in his family tradition also became a sergeant in the Grenadier Guards after the war.

Glad as I was to be home and away from the turmoil of war, I found it somehow rather strange and disturbing at times. I would at first find myself walking in the middle of the road, being unused to pavements and unconsciously adopting the habits I had become accustomed to. I found that the civilians at home had a very distorted vision of the life of an infantry soldier in war. The prevailing idea was of smart soldiers spending all their time standing in neat rows in a trench, facing the enemy, sometimes making spectacular bayonet charges for a change.

They did not realise that a soldier has to live and work as well as fight. There is no one to do his chores for him. In fact most of his time is spent in such unromantic occupations as carrying up rations, ammunition, barbed wire, duck boards and so on; digging and repairing trenches, fixing barbed wire entanglements, digging drainage sumps and latrines, priming hand grenades, sentry duty on the fire-step, going on night patrols or listening posts in no-man's-land, bombing raids, and so on when in the line. When back in reserve for a few days there would be drilling and training, guard duties and carrying parties during the night, taking food and stores up to the support lines. The so-called 'rest period' was in name only. Sometimes it was more restful in the trenches, if more dangerous.

This was a very different life from that conjured up in the civilian's imagination. Nowadays I suppose the general public have become much more sophisticated in this respect, having gleaned much information from films and television of actual events and conditions. I found it irritating to mix with civilian men, feeling that those who had been in the services were a different breed, with nothing in common with me. They did not belong to the great brotherhood and could not possibly understand us. I thought that my spirit would always remain in France where the flower of my generation had bled into the soil of Flanders. After over half a century I still get this feeling at times. Also I felt disappointed that I had been unable to take part in the final victorious advance and the liberation of France. It was a long time before this obsession grew thin.

As regards my future, both my mother and I had been warned that I would probably not enjoy a long life. How wrong this assumption was to be. In spite of having originally a rather groggy left lung, now perforated, aspirated and subjected to heavy chain-smoking since schooldays, I am still going strong in my eightieth year. I had always detested working in an office, and after four years of open air life was inclined to find an outdoor occupation. However this was not easy, not only because my wounds had not as yet reached a stage to stand much physical exertion, but jobs were very difficult to obtain and it was imperative for me to earn my living, there being no generous dole in those days. I was reluctantly persuaded to return to my old job in the office of an East Indian Export Agent in the Strand. I had made several enquiries about emigrating to Australia and for posts in West Africa and the Middle East, but to no avail. One had to have some capital for

Australia or South Africa, and companies in other countries had their own staff of young men trained for posts abroad.

I was asked to report to my old office on the morning of 11th November 1918 to commence work. On the way I heard that the Armistice had been signed. Arriving at Aldwych I found that I could not cross the Strand to my office directly across the road. The streets were lined deeply with cheering crowds, groups of hilarious flagwavers going by on the tops of taxis and other vehicles. People were dancing in the side streets and London was in chaos. Passing the Duke of Wellington pub in the Strand, a favourite haunt of the Australians, I felt tempted to get a drink, but the bar was packed with drunken Aussies, shouting and throwing glasses about. The sounds of smashing glass deterred me and I decided that discretion was the better part of valour, so made my way through the throng to Leicester Square. Crowds of people were pouring out of Charing Cross and Leicester Square stations. Girls were grabbing at men, kissing and dancing with them – I had to undergo some of this treatment, and decided to make my way home as it seemed there would be difficulty in getting back later on when the crowds tried to wend their way homewards.

I joined the Regimental Old Comrades Association and with my father and uncle attended many of the Annual reunion dinners and other functions, meeting many of my old comrades. One of the stretcher bearers whose face I did not remember, and the Company QM Sergeant who said he had stepped over my body at Beaurains, were surprised to see me, as they both thought that I was finished and would not survive to get home.

I was still to be of some assistance to the Regiment, drawing the campaign maps for our 2nd battalion's part in our regimental history. The 1st Battalion's maps (France) had already been prepared, otherwise I would have been delighted to have drawn these.

I must end my narrative here, at the finish of what I consider the second stage of my life. My entry back to normality was made delightful by my mother, father and sister, and we spent several beautiful holidays in the Isle of Wight, which were to be shared a few years later by my sweetheart, soon to become my wife. But that is another story. When my daughter Pamela and I made our short visit to France a few years ago we were able to visit some of the old and well remembered sites. Perhaps I may be able to do likewise with my other daughter Joan some day, time and energy permitting.

'Greater love hath no man ...'

Brief Re-union

A young man stood by the railway line at London's Leicester Square, with bowler hat, brolly and briefcase. I last remembered the youth, a signaller, dragging his khaki form through the grey slime of 'Lousy Wood', his face haggard and white with exhaustion, a haunting fear in his eyes, but dogged determination in his movements. For days and nights without respite he and his comrades carried out their hopeless task, searching for the broken wires that linked the unit to brigade. No sooner were the breaks repaired than Jerry's shells once more destroyed their efforts to maintain liaison with the rear. Terror filled the air, short silences broken at intervals by the whine and shriek of approaching demons ending with horrible roars and crunches as shells erupted tearing craters in the already tortured ground, clods and debris flying upwards to scatter down again onto the shuddering earth. A putrid smell of corruption and explosives assailed the nostrils. Flesh and bones of both living and dead were torn and shattered. Nerves were stretched to breaking point as the hellish maelstrom had its way. At times a raving man would rush headlong away, or another would sit quietly sobbing. If fortunate such would be sent back as shell-shock cases. There was no relief – men would drop with exhaustion into the mud of some hole or corner and mercifully lose consciousness for a short while in fitful sleep, only to awake once more to the horrors ahead.

The day's ration was often only a hard biscuit, a lump of cheese and half-a-pint of water foul with chloride and petrol.

What made men face up to such conditions? Was it because there was no escape, loyalty to their comrades, pride in their country, the fear and disgrace of losing their manhood?

'Hello! How are you? What are you doing now? Oh! here comes my train – glad to have seen you again – good-bye.'

The crowd jostles forward unaware of the sacred bond just re-awakened between these two 'ancient' young men.

Epilogue

Now that my reminiscences have been committed to paper the sense of realism has mysteriously disappeared, events becoming almost dreamlike. The wound scars are there to convince me, but even these are becoming faint with the passing of time. Nevertheless the memory of fallen comrades will always remain clear and bitter-sweet.

These four years witnessed the destruction of the flower of the finest generation ever to grace our nation. I pay homage to all those young men of whatever nationality who chose to go forward, often time and again, into the furnaces of hell in order to uphold their beliefs in the righteousness of their cause. These men bore no personal enmity against their neighbours and would have been content to live in peace. The culprits were the ambitious rulers grasping for yet more power, the greedy financiers and industrialists, and the misguided and often ignorant politicians. Millions of their pawns were killed and maimed. Dreadful although the experience was, I would not have missed it. I am grateful that I was privileged to be able to take even my small share in the ordeal.

The recuperative powers and resilience of the human being are remarkable, as proved by thousands of old service men who years later volunteered to face war once more, although now aged and often disabled. Eventually all civilians, especially those dwelling in cities, had no choice but to endure the hardships and bombing, neither men, women nor children, the helpless and invalids included.

Perhaps the greatest sufferers were those mothers who had given birth to and nurtured their sons through years of loving care, only to lose them unnecessarily, not through the normal hazards of accident or illness, but by the deliberate and violent decisions of those in power.

'We shall remember them.'

Index